LUKE CARTER

INSTANT POT ASIAN COOKBOOK

Flavorful Asian-Inspired Recipes Made
Easy with Your Instant Pot (2024)

Copyright © 2023 by Luke Carter

All rights reserved. No part of this publication may be reproduced, stored or transmitted in any form or by any means, electronic, mechanical, photocopying, recording, scanning, or otherwise without written permission from the publisher. It is illegal to copy this book, post it to a website, or distribute it by any other means without permission.

First edition

This book was professionally typeset on Reedsy.
Find out more at reedsy.com

Contents

1	Introduction:	1
2	Chapter 1: Indian Instant Pot Recipes	2
3	Chapter 2: Thai Instant Pot Recipes	31
4	Chapter 3: Chinese Instant Pot Recipes	65
5	Chapter 4: Vietnamese Instant Pot Creations	85
6	Chapter 5: Korean Instant Pot Recipes	99
7	In summary:	107

1

Introduction:

At its core, the Instant Pot functions as an electric pressure cooker, offering a versatile solution for quick food preparation. This innovative kitchen appliance generates steam pressure to create a high-temperature environment, significantly reducing cooking times. Unsurprisingly, pressure cooking stands out as its primary and most frequently used feature.

Expanding on the Instant Pot's capabilities, it serves as a genuine multicooker, capable of sautéing and browning food akin to a stovetop skillet. Additionally, it excels in steaming delicate items like fish, eggs, and vegetables, and even operates as a yogurt maker. What sets the Instant Pot apart is its unique combination of high pressure and heat, enabling the preparation of dishes that traditionally demand hours of cooking in a mere fraction of the time.

Furthermore, Instant Pots are equipped with sensors that regulate internal pressure and temperature autonomously. The appliance only engages pressure cooking when its lid is securely sealed. Moreover, cleanup is simplified since all cooking is contained within a single pot, regardless of the dish prepared.

With the merits and functionalities of Instant Pots outlined, let's explore a variety of recipes from diverse cuisines that can be effortlessly crafted using this remarkable kitchen tool.

2

Chapter 1: Indian Instant Pot Recipes

The Instant Pot has simplified the art of cooking Indian cuisine, making it accessible for everyone to prepare delectable meals at home. An abundance of tantalizing Indian recipes is perfectly tailored for the Instant Pot, enhancing the cooking experience for enthusiasts. Within this section of the book, you will find recipes thoughtfully categorized as follows:

1) Vegetable and Paneer Creations

2) Bean and Lentil Delights

3) Meat, Seafood, and Egg Wonders

1.1 Vegetable and Paneer Creations (6-7 Recipes)

Paneer Butter Masala

Servings: 4
  Time Taken: 30 minutes

CHAPTER 1: INDIAN INSTANT POT RECIPES

Ingredients:

- 1 pound Paneer chunks
    - 1 teaspoon Cumin seeds
    - 1 Chili pepper
    - 1 large Onion, chopped
    - 2 tablespoons Butter
    - 1 tablespoon minced Ginger
    - 1 tablespoon minced Garlic
    - 4 large Tomatoes, chopped
    - 1/4 cup Cashews
    - 2 tablespoons Dried Fenugreek leaves
    - 1/4 cup Water
    - 1/4 cup Heavy whipping Cream
    - 1 tablespoon Honey
    - 1 teaspoon Salt (or to taste)

Condiments:

- 1/2 teaspoon Ground Turmeric
    - 1 teaspoon Coriander powder
    - 1/2 teaspoon Ground Cumin
    - 1 teaspoon Cayenne powder

Whole Condiments:

- 2 Cinnamon sticks
    - 5 Green Cardamom pods
    - 2 Black Cardamom pods
    - 1 teaspoon Black Peppercorns
    - 1 teaspoon Cloves

Instructions:

1. Prepare a spice pouch by bundling whole condiments in cheesecloth.
2. Combine all ingredients, excluding paneer, cream, and honey, along with the spice pouch in the Instant Pot. Seal the lid and set to manual or pressure mode at high pressure for 8 minutes.
3. After natural pressure release, remove the spice pouch and blend the contents until smooth. Add cream and honey, stir well.
4. Add paneer chunks and let the sauce rest for 5 minutes, covered.
5. Garnish with dry fenugreek leaves or cilantro before serving.

Eggplant and Potato Curry

Servings: 6
Time Taken: 24 minutes

Ingredients:

- 2.5 tablespoons Cooking oil
    - 1 cup finely chopped Onions
    - 1 cup chopped Bell peppers
    - 1 finely chopped Green chili
    - 5 grated Garlic cloves
    - 1-inch grated Ginger
    - 4 medium-sized Tomatoes
    - 10 Raw cashews (soaked and drained)
    - 9 Baby eggplants (halved)
    - 3 medium-sized Potatoes (quartered)
    - 1/3 cup Vegetable broth
    - 1 teaspoon Cumin seeds
    - 1 teaspoon Turmeric powder

- 1 teaspoon Coriander powder
- 1 teaspoon Garam masala
- 2 teaspoons Powdered Cayenne pepper
- Salt (to taste)
- Fistful of finely chopped Mint leaves
- Fistful of finely chopped Coriander

Instructions:

1. Grind cashews and tomatoes to a paste.
2. Heat oil, sauté onions for a minute, then add ginger and garlic for 30 seconds.
3. Add green chilies and bell peppers. Add masalas and water.
4. Add pureed tomatoes, cover, and cook for 3 minutes.
5. Add potatoes and eggplants. Press cancel for sauté mode.
6. Seal the lid and cook at high pressure for 2 minutes.
7. Adjust seasonings if necessary before serving.

Palak Paneer

Servings: 4
Time Taken: 20 minutes

Ingredients:

- 1 pound Spinach or Palak
    - 2 cups Paneer (bite-sized cubes)
    - 1 tablespoon Oil
    - 1 teaspoon Cumin seeds
    - 1 Green Chili, chopped
    - 1 medium-sized Onion, chopped

- 5 cloves Garlic, chopped
- 1-inch Ginger, chopped
- 1 medium-sized Tomato, chopped
- 1/4 cup Water

Condiments:

- 1/2 teaspoon Ground Turmeric
- 1/2 teaspoon Powdered Red Chili
- 1 teaspoon Coriander powder
- 1 teaspoon Salt (or to taste)

Instructions:

1. Heat oil in Instant Pot's sauté mode. Add cumin seeds.
2. Add ginger, onions, green chilies, and garlic. Sauté for 2 minutes.
3. Add tomatoes and spices; cook for 2 minutes.
4. Add spinach, set Instant Pot to pressure or manual mode at high pressure for 2 minutes.
5. Blend contents until creamy. Add paneer and garam masala.
6. Palak Paneer is ready.

Dum Aloo

Servings: 3
Time Taken: 30 minutes

Ingredients:

- 10 Baby potatoes (peeled, cored from the top, saving the carved pieces)
    - 2 tablespoons Ghee
    - 1 large Onion, finely chopped
    - 2 teaspoons grated Ginger
    - 2 teaspoons grated Garlic
    - 2 pureed red Tomatoes
    - 1/2 teaspoon Ground Turmeric
    - 1/2 - 1 tablespoon Kashmiri powdered Red Chili
    - 1/2 - 1 teaspoon Garam masala
    - 1 teaspoon Kosher salt
    - 15 Cashews
    - 1/4 cup warm Milk
    - 1 tablespoon dried Fenugreek leaves
    - Chopped Cilantro (for garnish)

Instructions:

1. Set Instant Pot to sauté mode, add ghee and onions. Cook for 2 minutes.
2. Add ginger, garlic, cut-out potato pieces, tomato puree, powdered red chili, garam masala, turmeric, and salt. Cook for 2 minutes.
3. Fill potatoes with the prepared gravy. Add 1/2 cup of water, seal the lid, set to pressure cook mode (High) for 8 minutes, then quick release pressure.
4. Add dried fenugreek, cilantro, and cashew paste. Switch to sauté mode and combine.
5. Bring to a boil, then turn off the Pot.

Lentil and Vegetable Khichdi

Servings: 3
Time Taken: 20 minutes

Ingredients:

- 1/2 cup Split green Moong lentils
  - 1/2 cup White Rice (washed)
  - 3 cups Water
  - 1 tablespoon Ghee
  - 1/2 teaspoon Cumin seeds
  - 1/2 tablespoon Ginger paste
  - 1/2 small Onion, chopped
  - 1 chopped Tomato
  - Cilantro (for garnish)
  - 1 small Potato (chopped)
  - 1/2 cup Carrot (sliced)
  - 1/2 cup Green peas

Condiments:

- 1/4 teaspoon Ground Turmeric
  - 1/4 teaspoon Cayenne powder
  - 1 teaspoon Salt

Instructions:

1. In sauté mode, heat ghee

. Add cumin and ginger, onions; cook for 1 minute.
   2. Add vegetables and condiments.
   3. Add lentils, rice, and water.

4. After the Pot beeps, conduct a natural pressure release.
5. Garnish with cilantro.

Mushroom Masala

Servings: 3
Time Taken: 30 minutes

Ingredients:

- 1/2 large Onion, chopped
    - 5 cloves Garlic
    - 1 inch Ginger
    - 1/2 to 1 Green chili
    - 1 teaspoon Oil
    - 2 Large Tomatoes
    - 1/2 to 1 teaspoon Garam masala
    - 1/2 teaspoon Paprika
    - 1/4 teaspoon Turmeric
    - 1 teaspoon Dried fenugreek
    - 8 ounces White mushrooms (sliced)
    - 1/2 teaspoon Salt
    - 1/2 cup Peas
    - 1 cup Chopped spinach
    - 1/4 teaspoon Sugar
    - 1/4 cup Raw cashews (soaked for 15 minutes)
    - 1/4 teaspoon Cayenne Powder
    - Cilantro (for garnish)

Instructions:

1. Blend onions, chilies, garlic, and ginger with water until a puree forms.
2. Add oil. When hot, add onion puree. Cook for 3 minutes.
3. Blend tomatoes until smooth.
4. Add spices, then tomato puree; blend.
5. Add mushrooms and salt; sauté for 6 minutes.
6. Press cancel for Sauté mode. Cook on high pressure for 6 minutes.
7. Add spinach, cashew cream, peas, cayenne pepper, and sugar.
8. Boil in sauté mode, garnish with lemon juice and cilantro.

Potato and Cauliflower Stir Fry

Servings: 4
Time Taken: 20 minutes

Ingredients:

- 1 medium Cauliflower (chopped into florets)
- 1 Potato (chopped into small cubes)
- 2 tablespoons Ghee
- 1 teaspoon Cumin seeds
- 1 Green Chili (split)
- 1/2 small Onion (diced)
- 1 large Tomato (chopped)
- 1/2 tablespoon minced Ginger
- 1/2 tablespoon minced Garlic
- 1 teaspoon Dry Mango powder
- Cilantro (for garnishing)

Condiments:

- 1/2 teaspoon Ground Turmeric
    - 1/2 teaspoon Cayenne powder
    - 1 teaspoon Coriander powder
    - 1/2 teaspoon Garam Masala
    - 1/2 teaspoon Salt (or to taste)

Instructions:

1. Heat ghee. Add cumin and green chili; sauté for 30 seconds.
2. Add onions and ginger-garlic paste.
3. Add tomatoes and spices. Add cubed potatoes; sauté for 2 minutes.
4. Add cauliflower florets.
5. Ensure all contents stuck at the bottom are included.
6. Garnish with cilantro and dry mango.

Chapter 1.2: Instant Pot Recipes for Meat, Eggs, and Seafood (8-9 Recipes)

Butter Chicken

Servings: 4
Time Taken: 25 minutes

Ingredients:

- 14 ounces Canned Tomatoes
    - 5-6 cloves Garlic
    - 1-2 teaspoons minced Ginger
    - 1 teaspoon Turmeric
    - 1/2 teaspoon Cayenne Pepper
    - 1 teaspoon Smoked Paprika

- 1 teaspoon Kosher Salt
- 1 teaspoon Garam Masala
- 1 teaspoon Ground Cumin
- 1 pound Boneless and skinless Chicken Thighs
- 4 ounces Butter cubes
- 4 ounces Heavy Cream
- 1 teaspoon Garam Masala
- 1/4-1/2 cup chopped Cilantro

Instructions:

1. Put all ingredients except butter, cream, and a teaspoon of garam masala in the Instant Pot.
2. Close the Pot, set the timer to 10 minutes of high pressure.
3. Open the Pot, remove chicken, set aside.
4. Add butter, cilantro, garam masala, cream, stir until incorporated.
5. For a thicker consistency, cool the sauce before adding cream and butter.
6. Reincorporate chicken, let it heat.
7. Serve with rice or zucchini noodles.

Chicken Biryani

Servings: 8
Time Taken: 1 hour 20 minutes

Ingredients:

For Marinating:
- 2 teaspoons Garam Masala
- 1 tablespoon grated Ginger
- 1 tablespoon minced Garlic

CHAPTER 1: INDIAN INSTANT POT RECIPES

- 1 tablespoon Powdered Red Chili
- 1/2 teaspoon Turmeric
- 1/4 cup Mint leaves
- 1/4 cup chopped Cilantro
- 2 tablespoons Lemon juice
- 0.75 cup Plain Yogurt
- 2 teaspoons Kosher Salt
- 2 pounds Whole bone-in chicken, skinless (cut into 12 pieces)

Other Ingredients:

- 3 cups Extra-long grain Basmati rice (soaked for 20 minutes)
  - 3 tablespoons Ghee
  - 2 Large Yellow onions (thinly sliced)
  - 2 Bay leaves
  - 2 teaspoons Salt
  - 1 teaspoon Saffron mixed with 1 tablespoon lukewarm milk
  - Eggs (boiled and shelled)
  - 1 Jalapeno (sliced into 8 pieces)

Instructions:

1. Prepare marinade, coat chicken, set aside.
2. In 'Sauté' mode, add onions and 2 tablespoons of ghee.
3. Cook onions until golden brown, set aside a portion for garnish.
4. Add 1 tablespoon of ghee, jalapenos, bay leaves, half of marinated chicken, and its juices.
5. For bone-in chicken, seal the Pot, shift valve to 'Sealed', set Pressure Cook time to 4 minutes.
6. Drain rice, add it gently onto chicken. Add 2 teaspoons salt and 3 cups water.
7. Seal Pot, set Pressure Cook timer to 6 minutes.
8. Open Pot, mix rice with chicken at the bottom.

9. Garnish with reserved onions.
10. Serve with Raita and lemon wedges.

Chicken Curry

Servings: 4
Time Taken: 30 minutes

Ingredients:

- 1 pound Boneless Chicken (cut into 1-2 inch pieces)
    - 3 tablespoons Ghee
    - 1 small Green Chili (chopped)
    - 1 inch Ginger (finely chopped)
    - 5 cloves Garlic (finely chopped)
    - 1 medium-sized Onion (finely chopped)
    - 2 medium-sized Tomatoes (finely chopped)
    - 1/3 cup Water
    - 1 tablespoon Lemon juice
    - 1/4 cup Cilantro (to garnish)

Whole Condiments:

- 1 Black Cardamom
    - 2 Bay leaves
    - 6 Cloves
    - 6 Black Peppercorns
    - 1/2 teaspoon Cumin seeds

Other Condiments:

- 2 teaspoons Coriander powder
    - 1/2 teaspoon Powdered Kashmiri red chili
    - 1/2 teaspoon Garam masala
    - 1/4 teaspoon Ground Turmeric
    - 1 teaspoon Salt

Instructions:

1. Heat ghee, add whole condiments, sauté for 30 seconds.
2. Add green chili, ginger, onions, and garlic; sauté for 4 minutes until brown.
3. Add tomatoes and spices, sauté for 4 more minutes.
4. Add chicken, sauté for 3-4 minutes.
5. Add water, deglaze pot. Cook under high pressure for 5 minutes.
6. Mix in lemon juice, garnish with cilantro.
7. Serve hot.

Chicken Tikka Masala

Servings: 4
Time Taken: 30 minutes

Ingredients:

For Marinade:
- 1/4 cup thick Yogurt
- 3/4 tablespoon grated Ginger
- 3/4 tablespoon minced Garlic
- 1 tablespoon Lime juice

- 3/4 tablespoon Powdered Kashmiri red chili
- 1/2 teaspoon Ground Turmeric
- 1 teaspoon Garam masala
- 1 teaspoon Salt (or adjusted to taste)

Condiments for the Sauce:

- 1/2 teaspoon Garam masala
    - 1/4 teaspoon Powdered Kashmiri red chili
    - 1/2 teaspoon Ground Turmeric

To Prepare the Sauce:

- 2 tablespoons Ghee
    - 1 cup finely diced Onion
    - 1 teaspoon grated Ginger
    - 1 teaspoon minced Garlic
    - 1 cup canned Tomato Puree
    - 1/2 cup Water
    - 1/2 cup Heavy cream
    - 1 tablespoon Dried Fenugreek
    - Cilantro (for garnishing)

Instructions:

For Marinating:

1. Combine all marinade ingredients except chicken.
2. Add chicken, coat well, marinate for 30 minutes to 8 hours.

Brown the Chicken:

1. Under high pressure, cook chicken pieces until light brown on all sides.
2. Cut chicken into 2-3 inch pieces.

Preparation for the Sauce:

1. In remaining oil, add ginger, garlic, onions; sauté for 3 minutes.
2. Add water to deglaze.
3. Add pureed tomatoes, spices, extra marinade, chicken; mix well.

Cooking the Curry at High Pressure:

1. Cook under high pressure for 4 minutes.
2. Add fenugreek, cream, mix.
3. Garnish with cilantro.

Instant Pot Lamb Rogan Josh

Servings: 4
Time Taken: 45 minutes

Ingredients:

- 1 pound Leg of lamb (cut into cubes)
    - 1 Red Onion (chopped)
    - 4 cloves Minced Garlic
    - 2 teaspoons minced Ginger
    - 1/4 cup Full-Fat Greek Yogurt
    - 1 tablespoon Tomato Paste
    - 1/4 cup chopped Cilantro

2 teaspoons Garam Masala

- 1 teaspoon Smoked Paprika
    - 1 teaspoon Kosher Salt
    - 1 teaspoon Turmeric
    - 1/2 teaspoon Ground Cinnamon
    - 1 1/4 teaspoon Cayenne Pepper (or adjusted to taste)
    - 1/4 cup Water

Instructions:

1. Combine all ingredients in the Instant Pot.
2. Cook for 15 minutes under high pressure.
3. Allow 10 minutes natural pressure release, then manual release.

Instant Pot Mutton Masala

Servings: 4
  Time Taken: 35 minutes

Ingredients:

- 1 pound Mutton bone-in (1-2 inch pieces)
    - 3 tablespoons Ghee
    - 1 Green Chili
    - 1 large Onion (finely chopped)
    - 1/2 tablespoon minced Ginger
    - 1/2 tablespoon minced Garlic

- 1 medium Tomato (chopped)
- 1 tablespoon Lemon juice
- Cilantro (for garnishing)

Whole Condiments:

- 1/2 teaspoon Cumin seeds
    - 6 Black Peppercorns
    - 6 Cloves
    - 1 stick of 1-inch Cinnamon
    - 1 Bay leaf
    - 2 Black Cardamom

Other Condiments:

- 1/4 teaspoon Ground Turmeric
    - 1 teaspoon Powdered Kashmiri Chili
    - 2 teaspoons Coriander powder
    - 1 teaspoon Garam Masala
    - 1 teaspoon Salt

Instructions:

1. In heated oil, add whole condiments, sauté for 30 seconds.
2. Add green chili, ginger, garlic, onions; sauté for 4 minutes until lighter in color.
3. Add spices, chopped tomatoes; stir, sauté for 2 minutes.
4. Add mutton, sauté for 5 minutes.
5. Close the lid of the pot.
6. In 'meat' mode, cook under high pressure for 30 minutes.
7. Mix in lemon juice, garnish with cilantro.

Instant Pot Egg Curry

Servings: 4
Time Taken: 30 minutes

Ingredients:

- 6 Eggs
    - 2 tablespoons Ghee
    - 1 teaspoon Cumin seeds
    - 1 sliced Green chili
    - 1.5 cups diced Onion
    - 1/2 tablespoon minced Ginger
    - 1/2 tablespoon minced Garlic
    - 1.5 cups diced Tomatoes
    - 2/3 cup Water (divided)
    - 1/2 cup Coconut Milk
    - 1 tablespoon Lemon juice
    - 1/4 cup chopped Cilantro

Condiments

- 1/2 teaspoon Ground Turmeric
    - 2 teaspoons Coriander Powder
    - 1/2 teaspoon Powdered Kashmiri Chili (or adjusted to taste)
    - 1/2 teaspoon Garam Masala
    - 1 teaspoon Salt (or adjusted to taste)

Whole Condiments (optional):

- 1 stick Cinnamon
    - 2 Bay leaves
    - 1 teaspoon Black Peppercorns

- 2 Green Cardamom

Instructions:

1. In 'Sauté' mode, heat ghee, add whole condiments, cumin seeds.
2. Add onions, chili, garlic, ginger; sauté for 3 minutes.
3. Add tomatoes, spices; sauté for 2 minutes.
4. Place trivet and a steel bowl with eggs into the pot.
5. Under high pressure, cook for 8 minutes.
6. Carefully remove egg bowl and trivet.
7. Once eggs cool, create holes on the surface using a fork.
8. Add coconut milk, 1/3 cup water. Add peeled eggs back in sauté mode.
9. Simmer for 3 minutes.
10. Garnish with lemon juice and cilantro.

Coconut Shrimp Curry

Servings: 4
Time Taken: 20 minutes

Ingredients:

- 1 pound Shrimp (deveined with tail-on)
    - 1 tablespoon Oil
    - 1 teaspoon Mustard Seeds
    - 1 Green chili
    - 1 cup chopped Onion
    - 1/2 tablespoon minced Ginger
    - 1/2 tablespoon minced Garlic
    - 1 cup Tomato (chopped)
    - 1/4 can Coconut Milk

- 1 tablespoon Lime juice
- 1/4 cup chopped Cilantro (for garnishing)

Condiments:

- 1/2 teaspoon Ground Turmeric
    - 1/2 teaspoon Powdered Red Chili (or adjusted to taste)
    - 1/2 teaspoon Garam masala
    - 1 teaspoon Coriander powder
    - 1/2 teaspoon Salt (or adjusted to taste)

Instructions:

1. Add mustard seeds to oil; sauté.
2. Add green chili, ginger, garlic, onions; sauté for 5 minutes.
3. Add spices and tomatoes; sauté for 3 minutes.
4. Add shrimps and coconut milk; close the lid.
5. Run the Pot on low pressure for 3 minutes.
6. Drizzle the curry with lime juice, garnish with cilantro.
7. Coconut Shrimp Curry is ready.

1.3 Instant Pot Lentil and Bean Recipes (4-5 Recipes)

Instant Pot Dal Makhni

Serves: 4

Cooking Time: 55 minutes

Ingredients:

- 1 cup black gram lentils (rinsed and soaked for at least 4 hours or overnight)
    - 1/4 cup red kidney beans
    - 1 tablespoon butter
    - 1 teaspoon cumin seeds
    - 1 tablespoon minced ginger
    - 1 tablespoon minced garlic
    - 1 medium onion, diced
    - 2 medium tomatoes, diced
    - 3 cups water
    - 1 tablespoon lemon juice
    - Cilantro (for garnish)

Spices:

- 1 teaspoon powdered Kashmiri chili
    - 1/2 teaspoon garam masala
    - 1 teaspoon coriander powder
    - 1 teaspoon salt (or to taste)

For Brown Rice:

- 1 cup brown rice (rinsed)
    - 1.25 cups water
    - 1 tablespoon ghee
    - 1 teaspoon salt

Instructions:

1. Heat oil in the Instant Pot, add cumin seeds.
2. When they sizzle, add ginger, onions, and garlic. Sauté for 3 minutes.
3. Add spices and tomatoes. Sauté for 2 more minutes.
4. Add lentils, beans, and water. Cook under high pressure for 30 minutes.
5. Release the pressure and mix dal. Adjust consistency with water if needed.
6. Garnish with lemon juice and cilantro. Serve.

Instant Pot Dal Palak

Serves: 4
Cooking Time: 25 minutes

Ingredients:

- 1 cup split pigeon lentil (washed)
- 2 cups chopped spinach
- 1 tablespoon ghee
- 1/2 teaspoon cumin seeds
- 1 sliced green chili
- 1/2'' ginger, finely chopped
- 4 cloves garlic, finely chopped
- 1 large tomato, chopped
- 3 cups water

Spices:

- 1 teaspoon salt
    - 1/4 teaspoon ground turmeric
    - 1/4 teaspoon powdered red chili

Instructions:

1. Sauté green chilies, cumin, ginger, and garlic in heated oil for 30 seconds.
2. Add tomatoes and spices. Cook for 1 minute.
3. Add lentils and water. Pressure cook for 3 minutes.
4. Add garam masala and spinach. Sauté until spinach wilts.
5. Serve the spinach dal hot.

Instant Pot Chana Masala

Serves: 4
Cooking Time: 55 minutes

Ingredients:

- 1 cup chickpeas (soaked)
    - 1.5 cups water (for cooking)
    - 1 tablespoon ghee
    - 1 chopped green chili
    - 5 cloves minced garlic
    - 1 minced ginger
    - 1.5 cups diced onion

- 3/4 cup chopped tomatoes
- 1 tablespoon dried fenugreek leaves
- Cilantro (for garnish)

Spices:

- 1/2 teaspoon powdered red chili
  - 1 teaspoon coriander powder
  - 1 tablespoon chole masala
  - 1 teaspoon salt (or to taste)
  - 1 teaspoon dry mango powder

Whole Spices:

- 1 teaspoon cumin seeds
  - 2 bay leaves
  - 1/2 teaspoon black peppercorns
  - 1 stick cinnamon

Instructions:

1. Heat oil, add whole spices.
2. Sauté ginger, garlic, and onions. Cook for 3 minutes.
3. Add tomatoes and spices (except dry mango powder). Cook for 35 minutes.
4. Mash chickpeas for thicker sauce.
5. Boil for 2 minutes in sauté mode.
6. Garnish with cilantro. Serve hot.

CHAPTER 1: INDIAN INSTANT POT RECIPES

Instant Pot Green Moong Dal

Serves: 4
 Cooking Time: 30 minutes

Ingredients:

- 1 cup whole green lentils (rinsed)
    - 1 tablespoon ghee
    - 1 teaspoon cumin seeds
    - 1 chopped green chili
    - 1/2 tablespoon minced ginger
    - 1/2 tablespoon minced garlic
    - 1 medium onion, diced
    - 2 medium tomatoes, chopped
    - 3 cups water
    - 1 tablespoon lime juice
    - Cilantro (for garnish)

Spices:

- 1/4 teaspoon ground turmeric
    - 1 teaspoon coriander powder
    - 1/2 teaspoon powdered red chili
    - 1 teaspoon garam masala
    - 1 teaspoon salt

Instructions:

1. Sauté green chilies, cumin. Cook for 30 seconds.
2. Add ginger, garlic, onions. Cook for 1 minute.
3. Add tomatoes and spices.
4. Add lentils and water. Pressure cook for 15 minutes.
5. Add lime juice and cilantro. Serve hot.

Instant Pot Lobia Masala (Black Eyed Peas Curry)

Serves: 4
Cooking Time: 35 minutes

Ingredients:

- 1 cup black-eyed peas (soaked for 4 hours)
  - 1 tablespoon oil
  - 1 teaspoon cumin seeds
  - 1 medium onion
  - 1/2 tablespoon minced ginger
  - 1/2 tablespoon minced garlic
  - 1 green chili
  - 2 medium tomatoes
  - 2 cups water (for cooking)
  - 1 tablespoon lemon juice
  - Cilantro (for garnish)

Spices:

- 1/2 teaspoon ground turmeric
    - 1/2 teaspoon powdered red chili
    - 1/2 teaspoon coriander powder
    - 1 teaspoon garam masala
    - 1 teaspoon salt (or to taste)

Instructions:

1. Blend green chili, ginger, garlic, and onions into a paste.
2. Heat oil, add cumin seeds.
3. Add the paste, cook for 3-4 minutes.
4. Grind tomatoes. Add to the pot with spices. Cook for 3 minutes.
5. Add drained peas and water. Mix well.
6. Pressure cook for 12 minutes.
7. Add lemon juice and cilantro. Serve hot.

Indian Desserts Instant Pot Recipes (1 Recipe)

Milk Cake

Serves: 25
   Preparation Time: 2 hours

Ingredients:

- 15 ounces whole milk ricotta cheese
    - 1 cup sugar
    - 1/3 cup water
    - 1/2 cup ghee (at room temperature)
    - 2 1/2 cups powdered dry milk
    - 1 teaspoon fresh ground cardamom
    - 1 tablespoon chopped pistachios

Instructions:

1. In Instant Pot, mix sugar, ricotta, and water. Cook on high pressure for 11 minutes.
2. Add milk powder, cardamom, and ghee. Mix well.
3. Pour into an 8x8 container lined with parchment paper. Sprinkle pistachios.
4. Let it cool for 1 hour, then refrigerate for 3 hours.
5.

Slice into 1.5-inch squares. Serve chilled.

3

Chapter 2: Thai Instant Pot Recipes

Thai cuisine is renowned for its light yet spicy dishes. If the intricacies of Thai cooking have ever felt daunting, these Instant Pot recipes provide an effortless way to bring the rich and vibrant flavors of Thailand to your table.

2.1 Chicken Instant Pot Recipes (4 Recipes)

Thai Chicken Curry

Serves: 4
Cooking Time: 25 minutes

Ingredients:

- 1 1/2 pounds chicken breasts, cut into small pieces
    - 1/4 cup chicken stock
    - 1 can full-fat coconut milk
    - 1 tablespoon fish sauce (adjust to taste)

- 1 1/2 teaspoons fresh ginger or paste
- 2 to 4 tablespoons red curry paste
- 1 tablespoon lime juice
- 1 teaspoon lime zest
- Optional: 1 tablespoon brown sugar (adjust to taste)
- 1 medium onion, sliced
- 2 carrots, thinly sliced
- 1 red bell pepper, thinly sliced
- 1 yellow bell pepper, thinly sliced
- 1 cup snow peas
- Fresh cilantro (for garnish)
- Cooked rice (for serving)

Instructions:

1. In the Instant Pot, combine chicken stock, fish sauce, lime juice, coconut milk, curry paste, and lime zest.
2. Add chicken pieces to the pot.
3. Pressure cook for 5 minutes.
4. Remove chicken pieces with a slotted spoon and set aside.
5. In the pot, add onions, carrots, snow peas, and bell peppers.
6. Sauté for 3-4 minutes until the mixture boils.
7. Add chicken back to the pot and heat.
8. End sauté mode, transfer curry to a bowl, and garnish with cilantro.

Thai Lemongrass Chicken

Serves: 6

Cooking Time: 25 minutes

Ingredients:

- 1 can full-fat coconut milk
    - 1 small yellow onion, quartered
    - 4 cloves garlic, smashed
    - 1-inch piece fresh ginger
    - 1 tablespoon lemongrass paste
    - 1 tablespoon Thai red curry paste
    - 1 tablespoon fish sauce
    - Black pepper and kosher salt (adjust to taste)
    - 2 pounds boneless, skinless chicken breasts
    - 1 red bell pepper, chopped
    - 1 Fresno pepper, seeds removed, chopped
    - 1 cinnamon stick
    - 1/4 cup fresh cilantro, roughly chopped
    - 1/4 cup fresh basil, roughly torn
    - 1 lime, juiced
    - Shredded carrots, green onions, peanuts (for garnish)
    - Steamed rice (for serving)

Instructions:

1. Blend coconut milk, garlic, lemongrass, ginger, onions, curry paste, and fish sauce in a blender until smooth.
2. In the Instant Pot, combine coconut sauce, Fresno pepper, cinnamon stick, bell pepper, and chicken.
3. Pressure cook for 8 minutes.
4. Boil for 5 minutes in sauté mode.
5. Remove cinnamon stick. Shred chicken with forks.
6. Add basil, cilantro, lime juice, and salt. Mix well.
7. Serve chicken over rice, topped with carrots, green onions, and peanuts.

Thai Coconut Chicken Soup

Serves: 4
Cooking Time: 15 minutes

Ingredients:

- 2 tablespoons oil
    - 1 small onion, quartered
    - 2 pounds boneless, skinless chicken breast or thighs, cubed
    - 2 tablespoons red Thai curry paste
    - 1 red bell pepper, cut in thick strips
    - Optional: 6 slices galangal, torn kaffir lime leaves
    - 3 cups chicken broth
    - 2 tablespoons fish sauce
    - Salt (adjust to taste)
    - 1 tablespoon sugar
    - 3/4 cup coconut milk
    - 2 1/2 tablespoons lime juice
    - Cilantro leaves (for garnish)

Instructions:

1. Sauté onions for 10 seconds, then add chicken and sauté until white.
2. Add bell peppers, kaffir leaves, galangal, and Thai curry paste.
3. Add chicken stock, sugar, and fish sauce. Pressure cook for 6 minutes.
4. After pressure release, add lime juice and coconut milk.
5. Garnish with cilantro.

Thai Peanut Chicken

Serves: 4-6
Cooking Time: 25 minutes

Ingredients:

- 1-2 tablespoons canola oil
  - 2 pounds boneless chicken thighs, trimmed and skinless
  - 1/2 cup low-sodium chicken broth
  - 1/4 cup low-sodium soy sauce
  - 1 tablespoon dried and frozen cilantro or 3 tablespoons fresh, diced
  - 2 tablespoons lime juice
  - 1/8 to 1/4 teaspoon red chili flakes
  - 1 teaspoon ground ginger
  - 1/4 cup peanut butter
  - 1 tablespoon cornstarch
  - 2 tablespoons water
  - Cooked white rice (for serving)
  - 1/4 cup chopped peanuts
  - Green onions (chopped for garnish)
  - Lime wedges (for serving)

Instructions:

1. In heated oil, brown chicken in batches. Set aside.
2. Add chicken broth, cilantro, red pepper, soy sauce, ginger, and lime juice to Instant Pot. Mix.
3. Add peanut butter and seared chicken with juices.
4. Pressure cook for 9 minutes.

5. Remove chicken, leaving sauce.
6. In a small bowl, mix cornstarch in 2 tablespoons water.
7. Add mixture to sauce, stirring continually.
8. In simmer mode, boil sauce until thickened. Add chicken.
9. Garnish with green onions and peanuts.

2.2 Vegan/Vegetarian Instant Pot Recipes (5 Recipes)

Vegetarian Thai Red Curry

Serves: 4
Cooking Time: 20 minutes

Ingredients:

- 1 teaspoon oil
  - 1 medium onion, chopped
  - 1 red bell pepper, chopped
  - 1 cup baby corn, bite-size pieces
  - 1 cup firm tofu, cubed
  - 1 cup carrot, chopped
  - 1 cup zucchini, cubed
  - 1 teaspoon minced ginger
  - 1 teaspoon minced garlic
  - 1 tablespoon red Thai curry paste
  - 1 tablespoon liquid coconut amino
  - 1 tablespoon rice vinegar
  - 1 tablespoon brown sugar

- 1 can full-fat coconut milk
- 1 cup water
- 1 tablespoon lime juice
- Cilantro leaves (for garnish)

Instructions:

1. In the pot, add oil, garlic, ginger, and onions. Sauté until translucent and fragrant.
2. Add vegetables and tofu. Sauté.
3. Add water and stir.
4. Add soy sauce, coconut milk, rice vinegar, sugar, and curry paste. Stir.
5. End sauté mode. Pressure cook for 1 minute.//
6. After pressure release, add cilantro, Thai basil, and green onions. Stir.
7. Before serving, drizzle curry with lime juice.

Thai Green Curry

Serves: 4
Cooking Time: 25 minutes

Ingredients:

- 1 tablespoon oil
  - 2 to 4 tablespoons green Thai curry paste
  - 1 can coconut milk
  - 1 large yellow onion, sliced
  - 1 medium zucchini, sliced into 1/2-inch pieces

- 8 ounces cremini mushrooms, quartered
- 1.5 cups Thai eggplant, 1.5-inch cubes
- 1 teaspoon salt
- 1 cup snap peas
- 1 small orange pepper, 2-inch slices
- 1 tablespoon brown sugar
- 1 tablespoon soy sauce
- 1/2 lime, fresh lime juice
- 1/4 cup cilantro
- 1/4 cup Thai basil

Instructions:

1. Heat oil in the Instant Pot. Add green curry paste. Sauté for 30 seconds until fragrant.
2. Add coconut milk, zucchini, onions, eggplant, mushrooms, and salt. Mix well.
3. Cook at low pressure for 1 minute.
4. Add pepper and snap peas. Add soy sauce, lime juice, and brown sugar. Mix.
5. Continue cooking in sauté mode until boiling. Press cancel.
6. Garnish with basil and cilantro.
7. Allow to cook for 5 minutes to thicken before serving.

Vegan Panang Curry

Serves: 4
Cooking Time: 40 minutes

Ingredients:

- 1.5 tablespoons oil
  - 1 medium red onion, chopped
  - 1 inch ginger, chopped
  - 5-6 large garlic cloves, chopped
  - 1 green chili, sliced
  - 3 tablespoons Panang curry paste
  - 2 tablespoons peanut butter
  - 1 cup vegetable broth
  - 14 ounces canned coconut milk
  - 1/4 teaspoon turmeric powder
  - 2 teaspoons tamari
  - 2 teaspoons brown sugar
  - 1/4 + 1/8 teaspoon salt
  - 4 ounces firm tofu, cubed
  - 3-4 baby potatoes, cut into 1-1.5 inch pieces
  - 1 large carrot, chopped into rounds
  - 1 medium red bell pepper, sliced
  - 1/2 cup broccoli florets
  - 1/3 cup Thai basil
  - Zest of 1 lime
  - 1/2 tablespoon lime juice
  - Crushed peanuts

Instructions:

1. Heat oil, add ginger, garlic, and onions. Sauté until onions are softened (about 3 minutes).
2. Add green chili and peanut butter-curry paste mix. Cook for 30 seconds.
3. Add 1/2 cup vegetable stock to deglaze.
4. Add coconut milk, remaining stock, brown sugar, salt, tamari, and stir.

5. Add potatoes, tofu, carrots, and mix. Cover.
6. Cook on high pressure for 3 minutes.
7. In sauté mode, add broccoli and red pepper. Cook for 5 minutes.
8. Add lime zest, juice, basil, and peanuts.

Thai Coconut Curry

Serves: 7

Cooking Time: 30 minutes

Ingredients:

- 2 tablespoons coconut oil
  - 2 sliced green onions
  - 4 cloves minced garlic
  - 1 teaspoon grated ginger
  - 1 cup chopped carrots
  - 1 cup chopped broccoli
  - 1 cup chopped cauliflower
  - 1 cup chopped mushrooms
  - 3 tablespoons curry paste
  - 1 can diced tomatoes with juice
  - 1 can coconut milk
  - 1 can chickpeas, rinsed and drained
  - 1/4 teaspoon kosher salt
  - 2 cups chopped kale
  - Zested lime
  - 2 sprigs Thai basil

Instructions:

1. In heated oil, add green onions, carrots, and garlic. Sauté until soft, stirring occasionally.
2. Add curry paste and coat vegetables. Sauté until aromatic.
3. Add broccoli, cauliflower, mushrooms, chickpeas, tomatoes with juice, and coconut milk.
4. Pressure cook for 1 minute.
5. Let the Instant Pot sit undisturbed for 10 minutes after the cycle finishes.
6. Add kale, cover, and let it tenderize.
7. Garnish with lime juice and green onions before serving.

Thai Butternut Squash and Chickpea Curry

Serves: 6
   Cooking Time: 40 minutes

Ingredients:

- 15 ounces butternut squash
   - 2 cups soaked chickpeas
   - 1 can coconut milk
   - 1/2 cup spinach
   - 1 tablespoon Thai red curry paste
   - 1 tablespoon ginger-garlic paste
   - 1 red Thai chili
   - 2-3 tablespoons cilantro
   - 1 tablespoon coconut oil
   - Salt (to taste)

- 3 cups water

Instructions:

1. In heated oil, add red Thai chili and ginger-garlic paste. Fry for 8-10 seconds.
2. Add spinach, stir, and cook for 15 seconds.
3. Add red curry paste and 1/2 cup water. Cook until boiling.
4. Add butternut squash.
5. Add drained chickpeas.
6. Stir. Add vegetable stock and salt.
7. Pressure cook for 35 minutes.
8. In sauté mode, add coconut milk and chopped cilantro.
9. Cook for a minute before turning off the Pot.

Note: These recipes are crafted to retain the authentic Thai flavors while adapting to the ease of Instant Pot cooking.

2.3 Beef Recipes (4 Recipes)

❖ Thai Beef Stew

Serves: 8

Preparation Time: 30 minutes

Ingredients:

- 1 tablespoon of Olive oil
    - 1¾ pounds of Beef stew meat (trimmed of fat)
    - 1 medium Yellow onion (thinly sliced)
    - 2 cloves of Garlic (minced)

- 2 teaspoons of Ginger (minced)
- 1 can of full-fat Coconut milk
- 1 can of fire-roasted Tomatoes (unsalted)
- 2-3 tablespoons of Red Thai curry paste
- 1 1/2 tablespoons of Fish sauce
- 1 teaspoon of Lime juice
- 1 teaspoon of Sea salt
- 1 can of Green beans (freshly trimmed)

Instructions:

1. Heat the oil and brown the beef, adding ginger, garlic, and onions.
2. Add tomatoes, fish sauce, lime juice, salt, curry paste, and coconut milk.
3. Close the lid securely.
4. Select the 'Soup' function and cook for 15 minutes.
5. When done, release the pressure valve.
6. Switch to the sauté mode.
7. Add green beans and stew for 10 minutes or until tender.
8. Your soup is ready to be served.

❖ Thai Beef

Serves: 4
Preparation Time: 60 minutes

Ingredients:

- 1 pound of Beef Roast
    - 2 cups of Carrot chunks
    - 1/4 cup of Peanut Satay Sauce
    - 1/4 cup of light Coconut Milk (canned)

- 1 1/3 tablespoons of Soy Sauce
- 1/8 teaspoon of Salt
- 1/8 teaspoon of Black Pepper

Instructions:

1. In a bowl, mix water, soy sauce, coconut milk, and satay sauce.
2. Pour this mixture over the beef in the pot.
3. Add carrots to the pot.
4. Pressure cook for at least 35 minutes.
5. Shred the meat before serving.

❖ Thai Beef and Potato Curry

Serves: 4

Preparation Time: 40 minutes

Ingredients:

- 1 tablespoon of Coconut oil
- 1 ½ pounds of Beef chuck (cubed in 2-inch pieces)
- 1 large Onion (diced)
- 1 pound of Russet potatoes (cubed in 2-inch pieces)
- 2 cans of full-fat Coconut milk (15 ounces each)
- 1/2 cup of Beef broth
- 2 Bay leaves
- 3 tablespoons of Sugar
- 2 tablespoons of Fish sauce
- 1 tablespoon of Tamarind paste
- 1/4 cup of Crushed peanuts

Instructions:

1. In the warm coconut oil, brown half of the beef for 3 minutes, then set aside. Repeat.
2. Sauté onions to incorporate any caramelized bits of meat.
3. Add the beef, potatoes, and curry paste. Mix.
4. Add the stock, fish sauce, bay leaves, sugar, tamarind paste, coconut milk, and crushed peanuts.
5. Adjust salt to taste.
6. Serve when ready.

❖ Beef Pad Thai

Serves: 4
Preparation Time: 30 minutes

Ingredients:

- 2 tablespoons of Olive oil
    - 3/4 pound of Beef
    - 4 cloves of Garlic (minced)
    - 3 tablespoons of low-sodium Soy sauce
    - 1/2 cup of Pad Thai Jarred sauce
    - 1 ½ cups of Water
    - 7 ounces of Rice noodles
    - 1 cup of Carrot matchsticks
    - 1/2 each of Yellow and red peppers (sliced)
    - 4 Green onions (sliced)
    - 1/3 cup of Peanuts (chopped)
    - 1/3 cup of fresh Cilantro (chopped)

Instructions:

1. Add olive oil, beef, garlic, soy sauce, and Pad Thai sauce to the pot.
2. Cook under high pressure for 2 minutes.
3. Add half of the peanuts, bell peppers, and carrot matchsticks.
4. Wait for 5 minutes.
5. Serve the Pad Thai, garnished with the remaining peanuts and cilantro.

2.4 Shrimp Recipes (4 Recipes)

❖ Thai Coconut Red Shrimp Curry

Serves: 6

Preparation Time: 30 minutes

Ingredients:

For Marinating:
- 1/4 cup of Coconut milk
- 1 teaspoon of Cumin
- 1 teaspoon of Paprika
- 2 teaspoons of Curry spice
- 3 tablespoons of Lime juice (fresh)
- 1/2 teaspoon of Sea salt
- 1 teaspoon of grated Ginger
- 1 clove of minced Garlic
- 2 pounds of large, deveined and peeled Shrimp

For the Sauce:

- 2 tablespoons of Coconut oil
    - 1 small White onion (diced)
    - 2 teaspoons of grated Ginger
    - 2 cloves of minced Garlic
    - 1 28-ounce can of Diced tomatoes
    - 3 tablespoons of Red curry paste
    - 1 14-ounce can of Coconut milk
    - 1 teaspoon of Sea salt
    - 1/3 cup of chopped Cilantro

Instructions:

1. Whisk together lime juice, spices, coconut milk, ginger, garlic, and sea salt. Add shrimp and toss to coat.
2. In warm oil, sauté ginger, garlic, and onion for two minutes.
3. Add curry paste, coconut milk, salt, and tomatoes.
4. Pressure cook for at least 7 minutes.
5. Add shrimp and marinating juices.
6. Cook until the shrimps are no longer pink, about 2-5 minutes.
7. Serve, garnished with cilantro.

❖ Thai Shrimp Coconut Soup

Serves: 4
   Preparation Time: 25 minutes

Ingredients:

- 3 cups of Chicken broth
    - 1/2 pound of medium Shrimp (peeled and deveined, with tails on)
    - 1 cup of canned Straw mushrooms (undrained)
    - 1 13.5-ounce can of full-fat Coconut milk
    - 6 to 8 thin slices of Ginger
    - 2 whole Thai Red Chiles
    - 2 tablespoons of Fish sauce
    - 1 tablespoon of minced Lemongrass
    - 1 teaspoon of Honey
    - 1/2 teaspoon of Salt
    - Zest of 1 lime
    - Juice from 2 or 3 limes
    - Cilantro (for garnish)
    - Lime wedges (for serving)

Instructions:

1. Mix shrimp, chicken broth, mushrooms, liquid, ginger, half of the coconut milk, fish sauce, honey, lemongrass, salt, and chilies in the pot.
2. Cook under low pressure for at least 1 minute.
3. Stir in the remaining fish sauce, lime zest, coconut milk, and lime juice.
4. Garnish with cilantro and serve with lime wedges.

❖ Thai Egg Noodles with Shrimp

Serves: 3
Preparation Time: 25 minutes

Ingredients:

Pad Thai Homemade sauce:
- 2 tablespoons of Fish sauce
- 2 tablespoons of Soy sauce
- 2 tablespoons of Brown sugar
- Juice

of 1 Lime

- 2 tablespoons of Rice wine vinegar
- 2 tablespoons of Siracha
- 2 tablespoons of Olive oil
- 2 tablespoons of minced Garlic
- 2 cups of Water
- 8 ounces of Extra Wide Egg Noodles
- 1/4 cup of finely chopped Shallots
- 1 Carrot (chopped into matchsticks)
- 1/2 Yellow pepper (thinly sliced)
- 1/2 cup of baked or fried Cubed Tofu
- 1/2 pound of Skinned and deveined Shrimps
- 4 Green onions (sliced)
- 1/4 cup of Peanuts (chopped)
- 3 tablespoons of fresh Cilantro (chopped)

Instructions:

1. In the pot, sauté oil, garlic, and shallots for 3 minutes.
2. Add pad Thai sauce, carrots, yellow bell peppers, water, and egg noodles.
3. Pressure cook for 4 minutes under high pressure.
4. Add tofu and shrimp carefully.
5. Let it rest for 5 minutes; the shrimps will cook through the residual heat.

6. Serve, topped with cilantro and chopped green onions.

❖ Thai Shrimp and Sweet Potato Curry Soup

Serves: 4

Preparation Time: 21 minutes

Ingredients:

- 1/2 pound of Shrimp (deveined and peeled, paper towel-dried)
- 3 teaspoons of Soy Sauce (divided)
- 3 teaspoons of Honey (divided)
- 3 tablespoons of Vegetable oil (divided)
- 1 medium Sweet potato (peeled, cubed into 3/4-inch pieces)
- 3 tablespoons of Red Thai Curry Paste
- 1 14.5-ounce can of Chicken stock
- 1 13.5-ounce can of Coconut milk
- 2 handfuls of Baby spinach
- 1/4 teaspoon of Salt
- Cilantro (for garnish)

Instructions:

1. Mix shrimp with 1 teaspoon of soy sauce and 1 teaspoon of honey.
2. In the warmed Instant Pot, add shrimps and 1 tablespoon of oil.
3. Add remaining oil, cubed sweet potatoes, and Thai curry paste.
4. Sauté for 2 minutes, then add chicken stock.
5. Pressure cook in the soup mode for 5 minutes.
6. Release the lid, add coconut milk, remaining shrimps, soy sauce, honey, spinach, cooked shrimps with their juices, and salt.
7. Let the soup boil for 2 minutes.

8. Garnish with cilantro before serving.

2.5 Thai Desserts Instant Pot Recipes (3 Recipes)

❖ Thai Coconut Rice Pudding

Serves: 8
Preparation Time: 30 minutes

Ingredients:

- 2 cups of Dry jasmine rice
    - 4 1/2 cups of Unsweetened Coconut Milk (divided)
    - 2 tablespoons of Coconut cream
    - 2 tablespoons of Maple syrup
    - 2 teaspoons of Ground cinnamon
    - 1/2 teaspoon of Ground Turmeric
    - 1/2 teaspoon of Ground ginger
    - 1 1/2 teaspoons of Vanilla extract
    - 1/2 teaspoon of Coconut extract
    - 1/2 cup of Golden raisins

Instructions:

1. Mix dried jasmine rice with 3 1/2 cups of coconut milk in the pot.
2. Secure the lid, select the high-pressure setting, and cook for 3 minutes.
3. Once the rice is done, add maple syrup, coconut cream, ground cinnamon, ginger, turmeric, golden raisins, vanilla, and coconut extracts.
4. Top with golden raisins.

❖ Thai Mango Sticky Rice

Serves: 6

Preparation Time: 20 minutes

Ingredients:

- 3 small Mangoes
- 1 cup of Glutinous rice
- 2/3 cup of Water
- 1 can of Coconut milk
- 3/4 cup of Sugar
- 1 tablespoon of Cornstarch
- 2 tablespoons of Water

Instructions:

1. Place glutinous rice in a heatproof bowl inside the Instant Pot.
2. Pour 1/2 cup of water into the Instant Pot. Using a foil sling, lower the steamer rack with the bowl into the Instant Pot.
3. Pressure cook the rice for 13 minutes.
4. Simmer 2/3 cup of coconut milk over medium heat.
5. Add 5 tablespoons of sugar and 1/4 teaspoon of salt, whisking until well combined and the milk has a salty-sweet taste.
6. Pour the heated milk over the cooked rice.
7. Let it rest until the liquid is absorbed, around 20 minutes.
8. In a pan, combine the remaining milk with cornstarch, mixing until a smooth slurry forms.
9. Simmer the mixture in the pan over medium heat, whisking occasionally. Combine the slurry with the coconut milk on the stove, simmering for 2 minutes or until thickened.
10. Add the remaining sugar and salt until dissolved.
11. To serve, shape the rice into mounds on plates using a 1-cup measuring utensil. Arrange diced mangoes alongside the rice. Pour the warmed coconut cream over the rice and garnish with sesame seeds.

❖ Thai Triple Coconut Rice

Serves: 4

Preparation Time: 8 minutes

Ingredients:
- 1 1/2 cups of Jasmine Rice
- 1 can of Coconut Milk
- 1/2 cup of Water
- 2 teaspoons of Coconut Sugar
- 1 tablespoon of Coconut Cream
- 1/2 teaspoon of Sea Salt
- 1 splash of Vanilla Extract
- Toasted or Untoasted Coconut Flakes

Instructions:

1. Rinse the rice and add it to the Instant Pot.
2. Add coconut milk, sugar, vanilla extract, salt, and water.
3. Close the lid and choose the pressure cooking option.
4. Cook for 3 minutes at high pressure.
5. Allow the pressure to release naturally.
6. Fluff the coconut rice with a fork and garnish with coconut flakes.

2.3 Beef Recipes (4 Recipes)

❖ Thai Beef Stew

Serves: 8

Preparation Time: 30 minutes

Ingredients:

- 1 tablespoon of Olive oil
  - 1¾ pounds of Beef stew meat (trimmed of fat)
  - 1 medium Yellow onion (thinly sliced)
  - 2 cloves of Garlic (minced)
  - 2 teaspoons of Ginger (minced)
  - 1 can of full-fat Coconut milk
  - 1 can of fire-roasted Tomatoes (unsalted)
  - 2-3 tablespoons of Red Thai curry paste
  - 1 1/2 tablespoons of Fish sauce
  - 1 teaspoon of Lime juice
  - 1 teaspoon of Sea salt
  - 1 can of Green beans (freshly trimmed)

Instructions:

1. Heat the oil and brown the beef, adding ginger, garlic, and onions.
2. Add tomatoes, fish sauce, lime juice, salt, curry paste, and coconut milk.
3. Close the lid securely.
4. Select the 'Soup' function and cook for 15 minutes.
5. When done, release the pressure valve.
6. Switch to the sauté mode.
7. Add green beans and stew for 10 minutes or until tender.
8. Your soup is ready to be served.

❖ Thai Beef

Serves: 4

Preparation Time: 60 minutes

Ingredients:

- 1 pound of Beef Roast
- 2 cups of Carrot chunks
- 1/4 cup of Peanut Satay Sauce
- 1/4 cup of light Coconut Milk (canned)
- 1 1/3 tablespoons of Soy Sauce
- 1/8 teaspoon of Salt
- 1/8 teaspoon of Black Pepper

Instructions:

1. In a bowl, mix water, soy sauce, coconut milk, and satay sauce.
2. Pour this mixture over the beef in the pot.
3. Add carrots to the pot.
4. Pressure cook for at least 35 minutes.
5. Shred the meat before serving.

❖ Thai Beef and Potato Curry

Serves: 4

Preparation Time: 40 minutes

Ingredients:

- 1 tablespoon of Coconut oil
    - 1 ½ pounds of Beef chuck (cubed in 2-inch pieces)
    - 1 large Onion (diced)
    - 1 pound of Russet potatoes (cubed in 2-inch pieces)
    - 2 cans of full-fat Coconut milk (15 ounces each)
    - 1/2 cup of Beef broth
    - 2 Bay leaves
    - 3 tablespoons of Sugar

- 2 tablespoons of Fish sauce
- 1 tablespoon of Tamarind paste
- 1/4 cup of Crushed peanuts

Instructions:

1. In the warm coconut oil, brown half of the beef for 3 minutes, then set aside. Repeat.
2. Sauté onions to incorporate any caramelized bits of meat.
3. Add the beef, potatoes, and curry paste. Mix.
4. Add the stock, fish sauce, bay leaves, sugar, tamarind paste, coconut milk, and crushed peanuts.
5. Adjust salt to taste.
6. Serve when ready.

❖ Beef Pad Thai

Serves: 4

Preparation Time: 30 minutes

Ingredients:

- 2 tablespoons of Olive oil
    - 3/4 pound of Beef
    - 4 cloves of Garlic (minced)
    - 3 tablespoons of low-sodium Soy sauce
    - 1/2 cup of Pad Thai Jarred sauce
    - 1 ½ cups of Water
    - 7 ounces of Rice noodles
    - 1 cup of Carrot matchsticks
    - 1/2 each of Yellow and red peppers (sliced)

- 4 Green onions (sliced)
- 1/3 cup of Peanuts (chopped)
- 1/3 cup of fresh Cilantro (chopped)

Instructions:

1. Add olive oil, beef, garlic, soy sauce, and Pad Thai sauce to the pot.
2. Cook under high pressure for 2 minutes.
3. Add half of the peanuts, bell peppers, and carrot matchsticks.
4. Wait for 5 minutes.
5. Serve the Pad Thai, garnished with the remaining peanuts and cilantro.

2.4 Shrimp Recipes (4 Recipes)

❖ Thai Coconut Red Shrimp Curry

Serves: 6
Preparation Time: 30 minutes

Ingredients:

For Marinating:
- 1/4 cup of Coconut milk
- 1 teaspoon of Cumin
- 1 teaspoon of Paprika
- 2 teaspoons of Curry spice
- 3 tablespoons of Lime juice (fresh)
- 1/2 teaspoon of Sea salt
- 1 teaspoon of grated Ginger
- 1 clove of minced Garlic
- 2 pounds of large, deveined and peeled Shrimp

For the Sauce:

- 2 tablespoons of Coconut oil
    - 1 small White onion (diced)
    - 2 teaspoons of grated Ginger
    - 2 cloves of minced Garlic
    - 1 28-ounce can of Diced tomatoes
    - 3 tablespoons of Red curry paste
    - 1 14-ounce can of Coconut milk
    - 1 teaspoon of Sea salt
    - 1/3 cup of chopped Cilantro

Instructions:

1. Whisk together lime juice, spices, coconut milk, ginger, garlic, and sea salt. Add shrimp and toss to coat.
2. In warm oil, sauté ginger, garlic, and onion for two minutes.
3. Add curry paste, coconut milk, salt, and tomatoes.
4. Pressure cook for at least 7 minutes.
5. Add shrimp and marinating juices.
6. Cook until the shrimps are no longer pink, about 2-5 minutes.
7. Serve, garnished with cilantro.

❖ Thai Shrimp Coconut Soup

Serves: 4

Preparation Time: 25 minutes

Ingredients:

- 3 cups of Chicken broth
    - 1/2 pound of medium Shrimp (peeled and deveined, with tails on)
    - 1 cup of canned Straw mushrooms (undrained)
    - 1 13.5-ounce can of full-fat Coconut milk
    - 6 to 8 thin slices of Ginger
    - 2 whole Thai Red Chiles
    - 2 tablespoons of Fish sauce
    - 1 tablespoon of minced Lemongrass
    - 1 teaspoon of Honey
    - 1/2 teaspoon of Salt
    - Zest of 1 lime
    - Juice from 2 or 3 limes
    - Cilantro (for garnish)
    - Lime wedges (for serving)

Instructions:

1. Mix shrimp, chicken broth, mushrooms, liquid, ginger, half of the coconut milk, fish sauce, honey, lemongrass, salt, and chilies in the pot.
2. Cook under low pressure for at least 1 minute.
3. Stir in the remaining fish sauce, lime zest, coconut milk, and lime juice.
4. Garnish with cilantro and serve with lime wedges.

❖ Thai Egg Noodles with Shrimp

Serves: 3
Preparation Time: 25 minutes
Ingredients:

Pad Thai Homemade sauce:
- 2 tablespoons of Fish sauce
- 2 tablespoons of Soy sauce
- 2 tablespoons of Brown sugar
- Juice of 1 Lime
- 2 tablespoons of Rice wine vinegar
- 2 tablespoons of Siracha
- 2 tablespoons of Olive oil
- 2 tablespoons of minced Garlic
- 2 cups of Water
- 8 ounces of Extra Wide Egg Noodles
- 1/4 cup of finely chopped Shallots
- 1 Carrot (chopped into matchsticks)
- 1/2 Yellow pepper (thinly sliced)
- 1/2 cup of baked or fried Cubed Tofu
- 1/2 pound of Skinned and deveined Shrimps
- 4 Green onions (sliced)
- 1/4 cup of Peanuts (chopped)
- 3 tablespoons of fresh Cilantro (chopped)

Instructions:

1. In the pot, sauté oil, garlic, and shallots for 3 minutes.
2. Add pad Thai sauce, carrots, yellow bell peppers, water, and egg noodles.
3. Pressure cook for 4 minutes under high pressure.
4. Add tofu and shrimp carefully.
5. Let it rest for 5 minutes; the shrimps will cook through the residual heat.
6. Serve, topped with cilantro and chopped green onions.

❖ Thai Shrimp and Sweet Potato Curry Soup

Serves: 4
Preparation Time: 21 minutes

Ingredients:

- 1/2 pound of Shrimp (deveined and peeled, paper towel-dried)
    - 3 teaspoons of Soy Sauce (divided)
    - 3 teaspoons of Honey (divided)
    - 3 tablespoons of Vegetable oil (divided)
    - 1 medium Sweet potato (peeled, cubed into 3/4-inch pieces)
    - 3 tablespoons of Red Thai Curry Paste
    - 1 14.5-ounce can of Chicken stock
    - 1 13.5-ounce can of Coconut milk
    - 2 handfuls of Baby spinach
    - 1/4 teaspoon of Salt
    - Cilantro (for garnish)

Instructions:

1. Mix shrimp with 1 teaspoon of soy sauce and 1 teaspoon of honey.
2. In the warmed Instant Pot, add shrimps and 1 tablespoon of oil.
3. Add remaining oil, cubed sweet potatoes, and Thai curry paste.
4. Sauté for 2 minutes, then add chicken stock.
5. Pressure cook in the soup mode for 5 minutes.
6. Release the lid, add coconut milk, remaining shrimps, soy sauce, honey, spinach, cooked shrimps with their juices, and salt.
7. Let the soup boil for 2 minutes.
8. Garnish with cilantro before serving.

2.5 Thai Desserts Instant Pot Recipes (3 Recipes)

❖ Thai Coconut Rice Pudding

Serves: 8

Preparation Time: 30 minutes

Ingredients:

- 2 cups of Dry jasmine rice
    - 4 1/2 cups of Unsweetened Coconut Milk (divided)
    - 2 tablespoons of Coconut cream
    - 2 tablespoons of Maple syrup
    - 2 teaspoons of Ground cinnamon
    - 1/2 teaspoon of Ground Turmeric
    - 1/2 teaspoon of Ground ginger
    - 1 1/2 teaspoons of Vanilla extract
    - 1/2 teaspoon of Coconut extract
    - 1/2 cup of Golden raisins

Instructions:

1. Mix dried jasmine rice with 3 1/2 cups of coconut milk in the pot.
2. Secure the lid, select the high-pressure setting, and cook for 3 minutes.
3. Once the rice is done, add maple syrup, coconut cream, ground cinnamon, ginger, turmeric, golden raisins, vanilla, and coconut extracts.
4. Top with golden raisins.

❖ Thai Mango Sticky Rice

Serves: 6

Preparation Time: 20 minutes

Ingredients:
- 3 small Mangoes
- 1 cup of Glutinous rice
- 2/3 cup of Water
- 1 can of Coconut milk
- 3/4 cup of Sugar
- 1 tablespoon of Cornstarch
- 2 tablespoons of Water

Instructions:

1. Place glutinous rice in a heatproof bowl inside the Instant Pot.
2. Pour 1/2 cup of water into the Instant Pot. Using a foil sling, lower the steamer rack with the bowl into the Instant Pot.
3. Pressure cook the rice for 13 minutes.
4. Simmer 2/3 cup of coconut milk over medium heat.
5. Add 5 tablespoons of sugar and 1/4 teaspoon of salt, whisking until well combined and the milk has a salty-sweet taste.
6. Pour the heated milk over the cooked rice.
7. Let it rest until the liquid is absorbed, around 20 minutes.
8. In a pan, combine the remaining milk with cornstarch, mixing until a smooth slurry forms.
9. Simmer the mixture in the pan over medium heat, whisking occasionally. Combine the slurry with the coconut milk on the stove, simmering for 2 minutes or until thickened.
10. Add the remaining sugar and salt until dissolved.
11. To serve, shape the rice into mounds on plates using a 1-cup measuring utensil. Arrange diced mangoes alongside the rice. Pour the warmed coconut cream over the rice and garnish with sesame seeds.

❖ Thai Triple Coconut Rice

Serves: 4
Preparation Time: 8 minutes

Ingredients:

- 1 1/2 cups of Jasmine Rice
    - 1 can of Coconut Milk
    - 1/2 cup of Water
    - 2 teaspoons of Coconut Sugar
    - 1 tablespoon of Coconut Cream
    - 1/2 teaspoon of Sea Salt
    - 1 splash of Vanilla Extract
    - Toasted or Untoasted Coconut Flakes

Instructions:

1. Rinse the rice and add it to the Instant Pot.
2. Add coconut milk, sugar, vanilla extract, salt, and water.
3. Close the lid and choose the pressure cooking option.
4. Cook for 3 minutes at high pressure.
5. Allow the pressure to release naturally.
6. Fluff the coconut rice with a fork and garnish with coconut flakes.

4

Chapter 3: Chinese Instant Pot Recipes

In the past, cooking Chinese cuisine might have seemed like a task reserved for experts. However, with the advent of the Instant Pot, the landscape has changed. Below, you'll discover a variety of recipes, from dumplings to chicken gravies, all prepared in record time.

3.1 Chicken Recipes (5 Recipes)

Cashew Chicken

Serves: 4
  Preparation Time: 20 minutes

Ingredients:

- 1 pound of diced Chicken Breast
    - 1/2 cup of Low-sodium Chicken Stock
    - 3 tablespoons of Low-sodium Soy Sauce
    - 2 tablespoons of Rice Vinegar

- 2 tablespoons of Hoisin Sauce
- 1 tablespoon of Honey
- 2 teaspoons of Sesame Oil
- 1 teaspoon of minced Ginger
- 1 Clove of minced Garlic
- 1 tablespoon of Cornstarch
- 1/2 sliced Bell Pepper
- 1 1/2 cups of chopped Broccoli
- 1/2 cup of Roasted Whole Cashews
- Salt and Pepper (to taste)

Instructions:

1. In the Instant Pot, mix soy sauce, hoisin sauce, honey, garlic, ginger, chicken stock, and vinegar.
2. Season diced chicken with salt and pepper, then add it to the pot. Pressure cook for 6 minutes.
3. Set aside half a cup of the sauce and mix it with cornstarch. Stir this mixture into the chicken until it thickens.
4. Add red pepper and broccoli. Let it rest for 3 minutes until the vegetables soften.
5. Top with cashews before serving.

Sweet and Sour Chicken

Ingredients:

- 1 pound of cubed Chicken Breast
    - 1 tablespoon of Onion Flakes
    - 1/4 teaspoon of Garlic Powder

- 12 ounces of Sweet and Sour Sauce
- 8 ounces of Pineapple Chunks
- 1 head of Broccoli
- Tri-colored Onions and Peppers (frozen)
- 1 cup of Water
- 1 tablespoon of Brown Sugar
- Avocado Oil

Instructions:

1. Sear chicken cubes in heated avocado oil until browned on all sides.
2. Add brown sugar, sweet and sour sauce, and a cup of water to the pot. Pressure cook for 12 minutes.
3. Incorporate broccoli, peppers, and pineapple with its juice. Pressure cook for an additional 2 minutes.
4. Release the pressure and serve the chicken with brown or plain rice.

Mongolian Chicken

Serves: 6

Preparation Time: 40 minutes

Ingredients:

- 4 skinless, boneless Chicken Breasts (cut in cubes)
    - 2 tablespoons of Sesame Oil
    - 3/4 cup of Brown Sugar
    - 4 minced Garlic Cloves
    - 1 tablespoon of minced Ginger
    - 3/4 cup of Soy Sauce

- 3/4 cup of Chicken Broth
- 1 cup of chopped Carrots
- 1 teaspoon of Red Chili Flakes
- 1 tablespoon of Garlic Powder

Instructions:

1. Coat chicken cubes in sesame oil and sauté with garlic, ginger, and onions for 1-2 minutes.
2. Incorporate chicken pieces and stir for 3-5 minutes.
3. Add soy sauce, brown sugar, and chicken broth to the Instant Pot. Pressure cook for 3 minutes.
4. Garnish with scallions and sesame seeds. Serve hot with rice.

Chinese Chicken Wings

Serves: 6

Preparation Time: 16 minutes

Ingredients:

- 1/4 cup of Tamari Sauce
- 1/4 cup of Apple Cider Vinegar
- 1 teaspoon of Sriracha
- 2 teaspoons of Powdered Chinese Five-spice
- 1 tablespoon of Brown Sugar
- 3 minced Garlic Cloves
- 2 tablespoons of Sesame Oil
- 5 sliced Scallions (separated into greens and whites)
- 3 pounds of Chicken Wings (separated at joints)
- 1 cup of Water

- 1/4 cup of toasted Sesame Seeds

Instructions:

1. In a bowl, combine apple vinegar, Sriracha, brown sugar, tamari, powdered five-spice, garlic, scallion whites, and sesame oil.
2. Reserve 2 tablespoons of the sauce in a separate bowl.
3. Marinate wings in the sauce and refrigerate overnight.
4. Place wings in a steamer basket inside the Instant Pot. Pressure cook for 10 minutes.
5. Brush the chicken with some sauce and air fry for 3 minutes until crispy.
6. Garnish with scallion greens and sesame seeds.

3.2 Soup Recipes (3 Recipes)

Instant Pot Congee

Serves: 8
   Preparation Time: 40 minutes

Ingredients:

- 1 1/2 pounds of Chicken Thighs
    - 6 cups of Water
    - 1 cup of Long Grain Brown Rice
    - 1 2-inch piece of Ginger
    - 1 teaspoon of Salt
    - Soy Sauce

- Sesame Oil
- 3 Green Scallions
- Chili Oil with crunchy Garlic

Instructions:

1. In a heated Instant Pot, add chicken thighs skin-side down. Cook for 5 minutes.
2. Add water, rice, and ginger.
3. Close the lid and pressure cook for 30 minutes.
4. Separate chicken meat from bones and add it back to the congee.
5. Adjust salt to taste, garnish with soy sauce or chili oil.

Chinese Dumpling Soup

Serves: 6

Preparation Time: 30 minutes

Ingredients:

- 10 cups of Vegetable Broth
 - 4 medium thinly sliced Scallions
 - 1 slice of Deli Smoked Ham (1/2 inch thick, rind removed, sliced into matchsticks)
 - 2 tablespoons of Tamari
 - 1/2 teaspoon of Ground Ginger
 - 4 ounces of Chinese Chicken Dumplings

Instructions:

1. Pressure cook on sauté mode for 10 minutes.
2. Mix scallions, broth, tamari, ham, ginger, and soy sauce in the pot.
3. Cook until steam rises from the pot.
4. Add dumplings.
5. Stir before serving.

Chinese Noodle Soup

Serves: 6
Preparation Time: 10 minutes

Ingredients:

- 2 cups of finely diced Vegetables
    - 2 Green Onions (white parts)
    - 1/2 inch of minced Ginger
    - 1 teaspoon of White Chili Vinegar
    - 2 teaspoons of Chili Sauce
    - 1 tablespoon of Oil
    - 32 ounces of Vegetable Stock
    - 10 ounces of Baby Carrots
    - 1 teaspoon of Soy Sauce
    - 4 cloves of minced Garlic
    - 6 ounces of cooked Noodles (drained and cooked)
    - Salt and Pepper (to taste)

Instructions:

1. Select the sauté mode, add oil, garlic, ginger, onions, and carrots to the Instant Pot.
2. Add chili sauce, vinegar, soy sauce, and vegetable stock.
3. Pressure cook for 10 minutes.
4. Add cooked noodles.
5. Let it simmer and then serve.

3.3 Beef Recipes (2 Recipes)

Beef Short Ribs

Serves: 4

Preparation Time: 50 minutes

Ingredients:

- 3-4 pounds Short Beef Ribs
    - 1 cup Beef Broth
    - 1/2 cup Soy Sauce
    - 1/4 cup Brown Sugar
    - 3 tablespoons Nakano Garlic Rice Vinegar
    - 3 cloves Minced Garlic
    - 2 tablespoons Minced Ginger
    - 1/2 cup Diced Onion
    - 8 ounces Whole Button Mushrooms
    - 1 teaspoon Black Pepper
    - 2 Diced Red Chilis

Instructions:

1. Set the Instant Pot to high pressure sauté mode.
2. Brown the ribs on all sides in the pot.
3. Turn off sauté mode and add remaining ingredients.
4. Add mushrooms as garnish.
5. Restart sauté mode, add remaining ingredients, including mushrooms.
6. Pressure cook for 50 minutes.
7. Serve ribs with rice, drizzling the sauce on top.

Chinese Pepper Steak

Serves: 6
Preparation Time: 30 minutes

Ingredients:

- 1.5 pounds Beef Strips
    - 1 Green Bell Pepper (sliced thick)
    - 1 Red Bell Pepper (sliced thick)
    - 1/2 Onion (sliced thick)
    - 1/4 teaspoon Garlic Powder
    - 1 1/2 cups Beef Stock
    - 1/4 teaspoon Ground Ginger
    - 3 tablespoons Soy Sauce
    - 1/4 teaspoon Black Pepper
    - 2 teaspoons Brown Sugar
    - 1 tablespoon Cornstarch

Instructions:

1. Add beef, onions, and bell peppers to the Instant Pot.
2. Add spices, soy sauce, and brown sugar.
3. Pour beef stock into the pot.
4. Pressure cook for 15 minutes.
5. Switch to sauté mode.
6. In a separate bowl, mix 1/4 cup cold water with a tablespoon of cornstarch.
7. Add this to the pepper steak.
8. Simmer until the sauce thickens.
9. Serve over white rice.

3.4 Noodles Recipes (2 Recipes)

Vegetable Chow Mein

Serves: 6-8
Preparation Time: 15 minutes

Ingredients:

- 16 ounces Hakka Noodles
    - 1 cup Snow Peas (trimmed)
    - 1/2 cup Chopped Celery
    - 1 cup Broccoli Florets
    - 1 cup Thinly Sliced Cabbage
    - 1/2 cup Green Onions
    - 1/2 cup Thinly Sliced Bell Peppers
    - 2 Carrots (peeled, matchstick diced)
    - 4 cups Low-sodium Vegetable Broth

- 1 teaspoon Grated Ginger
- 1 teaspoon Grated Garlic
- 1 teaspoon Sesame Oil
- 1 tablespoon Vinegar
- 1 tablespoon Sriracha
- 1 tablespoon Ketchup
- 1 tablespoon Light Brown Sugar

Instructions:

1. In a bowl, combine soy sauce, vinegar, Sriracha sauce, vegetable stock, ketchup, sesame oil, and brown sugar.
2. Pour this sauce into the Instant Pot.
3. Place noodles, garlic, ginger, and other vegetables (except snow peas and broccoli) in the Instant Pot.
4. Pressure cook for 5 minutes.
5. Stir the noodles frequently, separating any clumps. Add snow peas and broccoli. Let it rest for 1 minute.
6. Garnish with green onions and sesame seeds.

Chicken Lo Mein

Serves: 6-8
Preparation Time: 14 minutes

Ingredients:

- 1 3/4 cups Chicken Broth
  - 8 ounces Uncooked Spaghetti
  - 1 1/4 pounds Boneless Chicken Thighs (skinless, bite-sized pieces)

- 2 1/2 tablespoons Low-sodium Soy Sauce
- 1 teaspoon Minced Garlic
- 1 tablespoon Brown Sugar
- 1 1/2 teaspoons Sriracha
- 1 1/2 teaspoons Minced Ginger
- 1/2 teaspoon Sesame Oil
- 1 bag Frozen Vegetables

Instructions:

1. Pour broth into the Instant Pot.
2. Arrange spaghetti in a criss-cross pattern to prevent sticking.
3. Layer chicken over spaghetti. Mix chili garlic sauce, brown sugar, soy sauce, garlic, ginger, and oil in a bowl.
4. Pour this blend over chicken thighs.
5. Pressure cook for 4 minutes.
6. Allow the pot to rest for 5 minutes.
7. Sauté vegetables.
8. Turn off the pot and serve Chicken Lo Mein.

3.5 Pork and Lamb Recipes (3 Recipes)

Chinese Pork

Serves: 4-5

Preparation Time: 7 minutes (plus marinating time)

Ingredients:

- 1.5 pounds Thinly Sliced Pork Loin
    - 1/3 cup Soy Sauce
    - 1/3 cup Hoisin Sauce
    - 1/4 cup Dried Red Wine
    - 1 tablespoon Sugar
    - 1/2 tablespoon Minced Garlic
    - 1/2 teaspoon Five Spice
    - 2 drops Red Food Coloring
    - 1 tablespoon Sesame Oil
    - 1 tablespoon Olive Oil

Instructions:

1. Marinate pork slices in a mixture of soy sauce, hoisin sauce, red wine, sugar, garlic, five spice, and food coloring overnight.
2. In the Instant Pot, heat sesame and olive oil. Add pork and sauté for 2 minutes.
3. Add remaining marinade.
4. Set to manual for 4 minutes.
5. Serve with rice.

Char Sui Pork

Serves: 8
  Preparation Time: 1 hour 25 minutes (plus marinating time)

Ingredients:

- 1/2 cup Honey
    - 1/2 cup Hoisin Sauce
    - 1/4 cup Soy Sauce
    - 1/4 cup Ketchup
    - 4 cloves Minced Garlic
    - 4 teaspoons Minced Gingerroot
    - 1 teaspoon Five-spice Powder
    - 1 Boneless Pork Shoulder Roast
    - 1/2 cup Chicken Broth
    - Cilantro (for garnish)

Instructions:

1. Combine honey, hoisin sauce, soy sauce, ketchup, garlic, ginger, and five-spice powder in a shallow dish.
2. Coat pork with marinade. Refrigerate overnight.
3. Add marinade and pork to Instant Pot. Add chicken broth.
4. Pressure cook for 75 minutes.
5. Shred pork using two forks.
6. Remove excess fat from juices.
7. Place pork back in the pot, set to low heat, and warm pork in sauté setting.
8. Serve garnished with cilantro.

Steamed Lamb Dumplings (Buuz)

Serves: 8
Preparation Time: 1 hour

Ingredients:

Wrappers:
- 2 cups Flour
- 2/3 cups Boiling Water

Filling:
- 1 pound Coarsely Ground Fatty Lamb
- 1 Minced Onion
- 2-3 cloves Minced Garlic
- 1

-2 teaspoons Pepper
- 1 teaspoon Caraway Seeds
- 1 teaspoon Salt
- 1-2 tablespoons Water

Instructions:

1. Knead flour and water into a smooth dough.
2. Rest dough under a damp towel for 30 minutes.
3. Coarsely grind lamb and mix with remaining filling ingredients.
4. Roll wrapper dough into a long snake-like shape and cut into two dozen pieces.
5. For each dumpling, place a small portion of lamb filling on a wrapper, crimping the edges to seal.
6. Steam dumplings in the Instant Pot for about 20 minutes.
7. Serve as a main course or appetizer.

3.6 Chinese Rice Recipes (3 Recipes)

Chinese Rice

Serves: 4
  Preparation Time: 30 minutes

Ingredients:

- 1 cup White Basmati Rice
  - 1 cup Vegetable Broth
  - 1/2 teaspoon Five-spice Powder
  - 2 teaspoons Sesame Oil
  - 2 teaspoons Soy Sauce
  - Fresh Cilantro
  - Chopped Spring Onions
  - Diced Chilies

Instructions:

1. Combine all listed ingredients in the Instant Pot and mix well.
2. Cook rice on high-pressure for 3 minutes with the 'keep warm' function.
3. This Chinese-style rice can be served as a main dish or side.

Teriyaki Chicken Rice

Serves: 4-5
  Preparation Time: 20 minutes

Ingredients:

- 2 medium-sized Chicken Breasts (chopped into 1-inch pieces)
    - 1/4 cup Low-sodium Soy Sauce
    - 1/4 cup Hoisin Sauce
    - 2 tablespoons Rice Vinegar
    - 4 cloves Minced Garlic
    - 1 tablespoon Grated Ginger
    - 2 Chopped Carrots
    - 1 1/2 cups Water
    - 1 cup Jasmine Rice
    - 1 Chopped Broccoli Head
    - 1 Chopped Red Pepper
    - 4 Sliced Green Onions
    - 1 tablespoon Sesame Seeds
    - 1 tablespoon Olive Oil

Instructions:

1. In the Instant Pot, add olive oil, chicken, 1/4 cup soy sauce, 1/4 cup hoisin sauce, rice vinegar, minced ginger, minced garlic, chopped carrots, water, and jasmine rice.
2. Cook rice at high pressure for 2 minutes.
3. Add red pepper, green onions, broccoli. Cover and let rest for 5 minutes.
4. Garnish with sesame seeds and green scallions before serving.

Sesame Ginger Rice

Serves: 8

Preparation Time: 18 minutes

Ingredients:

- 2 cups Water
    - 2 cups Rice
    - 2 tablespoons Grated Ginger
    - 1 teaspoon Toasted Sesame Oil
    - 1 teaspoon Kosher Salt

Instructions:

1. In the Instant Pot, add rice, ginger, water, sesame oil, and salt.
2. Cook rice on high-pressure for 3 minutes.
3. Once the pressure has been released, fluff the rice with a fork or spoon.

3.7 Chinese Desserts Recipes (2 Recipes)

Red Bean Milk Soup

Serves: 6-8

Preparation Time: 40 minutes

Ingredients:

- 1 cup Red Beans
    - 1/2 cup Glutinous Black Rice
    - 1 piece Dried Mandarin Peel
    - 2 liters Water
    - 90 grams Rock Sugar
    - 90 grams Slab Brown Sugar

Instructions:

1. Soak mandarin peels in water until softened.
2. Wash red beans and glutinous rice. Drain.
3. Add all ingredients to the Instant Pot inner container.
4. Press the 'Soup' button.
5. Once pressure is released, the beans will be cooked, but for a smooth soup, press "Sauté" and cook for an additional 20 minutes without the lid.
6. Your red bean dessert is ready.

Tofu Pudding

Serves: 6
Preparation Time: 15 minutes

Ingredients:

- 4 cups Soy Milk
    - 1/2 cup Water
    - 1 tablespoon Powdered Agar Agar

- 2 teaspoons Vanilla Extract
- 1/2 cup Sugar
- 1 tablespoon Ginger

Instructions:

1. In a separate pot, heat soy milk and mix it with agar mixture.
2. Add vanilla extract and blend well.
3. Pressure cook for 3 minutes.
4. Strain the mixture and refrigerate until set.
5. In a bowl, combine all syrup ingredients except ginger. Remove the ginger.
6. Top the tofu with syrup and serve.

5

Chapter 4: Vietnamese Instant Pot Creations

In the realm of Vietnamese cuisine, where the art of crafting savory stews can often delve into complexity, the Instant Pot emerges as the game-changer, simplifying intricate processes with its efficiency.

4.1 Pho Recipes (5 Varieties)

Beef Pho

Serves: 8
Preparation Time: 1 hour 20 minutes

Ingredients:

- 4 pounds Beef Bones
  - 1-2 Star Anise
  - 1 Cinnamon Stick

- 1 1/2 teaspoons Whole Coriander Seeds
- 6 Whole Cloves
- 1 tablespoon Salt
- 1 teaspoon Whole Black Peppercorns
- 1 Small Onion (sliced in chunks)
- 1 tablespoon Cooking Oil
- 4-inch Slices of Ginger
- 1 tablespoon Coconut Sugar
- 4 tablespoons Soy Sauce
- 5 tablespoons Fish Sauce

Toppings:

- 1/2 pound Beef Tenderloin
  - 12 ounces Rice Noodles
  - 4 Sliced Jalapenos
  - 2 cups Bean Sprouts
  - 1 cup Mint Leaves
  - 1 cup Thai Basil
  - Hoisin Sauce (as needed)
  - Sriracha (as needed)

Instructions:

1. Toast coriander, star anise, cloves, peppercorns, and cinnamon in a warm skillet.
2. Roast beef bones in the oven at 450 degrees for 20 minutes.
3. Sauté onions and ginger in heated oil in the Instant Pot until charred.
4. Add salt, soy sauce, roasted bones, fish sauce, pepper, and coconut sugar to the Instant Pot.
5. Pressure cook for 2 hours.

6. Boil soaked rice noodles for 45 minutes, then drain.
7. Slice beef thinly.
8. Remove excess fat from the broth after cooking.
9. Layer noodles, beef, and hot broth in bowls.
10. Garnish with mint leaves or Thai basil.

Chicken Pho

Serves: 4

Preparation Time: 30 minutes

Ingredients:

- 14 ounces Rice Noodles
    - 1 tablespoon Olive Oil
    - 1 Large Yellow Onion
    - 2-inch Piece of Ginger
    - 3 Cardamom Pods
    - 1 Cinnamon Stick
    - 1 tablespoon Coriander Seeds
    - 3 Star Anise Pods
    - 5 Cloves
    - 1 Fuji Apple (cut in chunks)
    - 1/2 cup Coarsely Chopped Cilantro Leaves
    - 6 Chicken Thighs
    - 3 tablespoons Fish Sauce
    - 1 tablespoon Sugar
    - 8 cups Water
    - 1 1/2 teaspoons Kosher Salt

Instructions:

1. Soak noodles in warm water while preparing the pho broth.
2. Sauté oil, ginger, and chopped onions in the hot Instant Pot for 4 minutes.
3. Add coriander, cardamom, cinnamon, cloves, and star anise. Cook until aromatic.
4. Add water, cilantro, apple, fish sauce, sugar, and chicken to the pot.
5. Pressure cook for 15 minutes.
6. Remove chicken from the pot. Season broth with salt and pepper.
7. Cool chicken, remove from bones, and place in bowls.
8. Garnish with desired toppings and hot broth.

Bo Kho

Serves: 9

Preparation Time: 1 hour 25 minutes

Ingredients:

- 1/2 teaspoon Oil
  - 5 pounds Bone-in Short Ribs
  - 1 Diced Yellow Onion
  - 1 1/2 teaspoons Madras Curry Powder
  - 2 1/2 tablespoons Ginger
  - 2 1/2 tablespoons Diced Tomatoes
  - 3 tablespoons Fish Sauce
  - 2 tablespoons Apple Sauce
  - 1 Large Lemongrass Stalk (cut in 3-inch pieces)
  - 2 Whole Star Anise
  - 1 Bay Leaf

- 1 cup Bone Broth
- 1 pound Carrots (peeled and chopped in 1-inch pieces)
- Kosher Salt

Instructions:

1. Heat oil in the Instant Pot; fry beef.
2. Transfer seared meat. Sauté onions until translucent.
3. Add ginger, tomatoes, star anise, bay leaf, curry powder, lemongrass, apple sauce, and seared beef.
4. Add broth.
5. Pressure cook for 50 minutes.
6. Add carrots, cook for 7 more minutes under high pressure.
7. Adjust seasoning with fish sauce if needed.
8. Stew is ready to serve.

Phở Tái Bò Viên

Serves: 4
  Preparation Time: 1 hour 15 minutes

Ingredients:

- 3 Oxtails
  - 3 Beef Marrow Bones
  - 1 3-inch Piece of Ginger (cut in half lengthwise)
  - 1 Large Yellow Onion
  - 1/4 cup Fish Sauce
  - 3-4 Beef Stock Cubes

- Condiments:

- 5 Whole Star Anise
    - 1 tablespoon Fennel
    - 1 tablespoon Black Peppercorns
    - 1 tablespoon Coriander
    - 1/2 Stick of Cinnamon
    - 1 tablespoon Whole Cloves
    - 1 Spice Bag

- Noodle Assembly:

- 1 pound Dried Rice Sticks
    - 1/3 pound Beef Sirloin
    - 1 package Asian Meatballs

- Garnish:

- 1/2 Yellow Onion (thinly sliced)
    - 3 Scallions (thinly sliced)

Instructions:

1. Char ginger and onions in an oven at 400 degrees for 15-20 minutes.
2. Toast spices and place them in a spice bag.
3. For the bone broth, combine spice bags, bones, fish sauce, and beef stock cubes in the Instant Pot.
4. Add water to the maximum capacity.
5. Pressure cook for 30 minutes and allow 30 minutes of natural pressure release.
6. Soak, drain, and cook rice noodles.

7. Layer noodles, meat, and meatballs in bowls.
8. Discard spice bags and bone marrow.
9. Pour prepared broth over meat.
10. Garnish with black pepper and serve.

Vegetarian Pho

Servings:
Time Taken:

Ingredients:

- 12 ounces Dried Rice Noodles
- 2 tablespoons Olive Oil
- 2 Large Onions (halved)
- 4-inch Piece of Ginger (halved)
- 2 Cinnamon Sticks
- 2 Star Anise
- 2 Whole Cloves
- 2 teaspoons Coriander Seeds
- 4 cups Vegetable Broth
- 4 cups Water
- 2 tablespoons Tamari
- 4 ounces Firm Tofu (chopped into 16 squares)

Garnishes:

- Cilantro
    - Thai Basil

Instructions:

1. Preheat the oven to 400 degrees.
2. Cook the rice noodles according to the package instructions.
3. In sauté mode, heat olive oil for 7 minutes.
4. Add cinnamon, onions, ginger, cloves, coriander seeds, and star anise. Stir until ginger and onions are slightly charred.
5. Add water, soy sauce, and vegetable stock.
6. Put on the lid and pressure cook for 15 minutes.
7. Bake tofu in the oven at 400 degrees for 25 minutes.
8. Release pressure and strain the broth using a mesh sieve.
9. In a bowl, combine tofu and noodles, then pour hot broth over them.
10. Garnish with cilantro and Thai basil.

Caramelized Pork

Servings: 6
   Time Taken: 50 minutes

Ingredients:

- 2 pounds Pork Shoulder (cut into 1-2" pieces)
    - 2 tablespoons Cooking Oil
    - 2 tablespoons Fish Sauce

- 4 tablespoons Brown Sugar
- 1 teaspoon Black Pepper
- 3 cloves Garlic (minced)
- 1/4 cup Pork Broth
- 1/4 cup Water
- 1 small Onion (sliced)
- Green Onions (optional, for garnish)
- Fried Shallots (optional, for garnish)

Instructions:

1. Heat oil and sear pork pieces until browned.
2. Add sugar and cook until golden brown, stirring constantly.
3. Add garlic and sauté for a minute.
4. Add remaining ingredients (except onions) and pressure cook for 15 minutes.
5. Switch to sauté mode, add onions, and cook until the sauce thickens (about 5-10 minutes).
6. Remove from heat and garnish with fried shallots and green onions.

Banh Mi

Servings:6
Time Taken:1 hour 25 minutes

Ingredients:

For Pork:

- 1 tablespoon Lime Juice
    - 1/4 cup Fish Sauce
    - 1/4 tablespoon Garlic (minced)
    - 1 teaspoon Black Pepper
    - 1 teaspoon Powdered Chinese Five-spice
    - 2 tablespoons Sugar
    - 2.5 pounds Pork Shoulder
    - 1 tablespoon Vegetable Oil

For Sandwich:

- French Baguette
    - Pâté
    - Pickled Julienned Daikon
    - Maggi Flavoring Sauce
    - Sriracha Mayonnaise
    - Sliced Jalapeno

Instructions:

1. For the pork, mix fish sauce, garlic, sugar, Chinese spice powder, lime juice, and black pepper in a bowl.
2. Coat pork with the mixture evenly.
3. Place pork in the Instant Pot and cook under pressure for 60 minutes.
4. Remove pork and shred it using forks; reserve the cooking juices.
5. Fry shredded pork in a nonstick pan using reserved juices.
6. To assemble the sandwich, cut the baguette in half lengthwise.
7. Spread mayonnaise on one end and pâté on the other.
8. Top with pork, Maggi sauce, pickled daikon, and jalapenos.

9. Banh mi is ready to be served.

4.3 Vietnamese Chicken Curry Recipe (Serves 4, Preparation Time: 15 minutes)

Ingredients:

- 6 boneless, skinless chicken thighs, halved
    - 1 tablespoon gluten-free fish sauce
    - 1 tablespoon gluten-free tamari sauce
    - 1 tablespoon gluten-free curry powder
    - Juice of 1 large lime
    - 2 cloves garlic, thinly sliced
    - 1 yellow onion, sliced into wedges
    - 3 large carrots, cut into 1-inch pieces
    - 1 pound Gold Yukon potatoes, cut into bite-size pieces
    - 1 yellow or red bell pepper, cut into bite-size pieces
    - 1/4 pound mushrooms, quartered
    - 2 lemongrass sticks, lightly smashed
    - 2 tablespoons honey
    - 2 cups gluten-free chicken stock
    - 1 bay leaf
    - 1 teaspoon sea salt
    - 1 can coconut milk
    - Fresh basil leaves, sliced jalapenos, and lime wedges for garnish

Instructions:

1. In a bowl, marinate the chicken with fish sauce, tamari sauce, curry powder, lime juice, and sliced garlic. Let it marinate for at least 15 minutes.
2. After marinating, place the chicken in the Instant Pot along with the marinating sauce.
3. Add all the vegetables, lemongrass, honey, chicken stock, bay leaf, and sea salt, excluding the coconut milk.
4. Close the Instant Pot with the lid and cook the chicken under high pressure for 12 minutes.
5. Once cooked, remove the bay leaf and lemongrass.
6. Stir in the coconut milk and cook in sauté mode for about 2 minutes.
7. Serve the curry hot, garnished with fresh basil leaves, sliced jalapenos, and lime wedges.

—-

4.4 Vietnamese Caramel Salmon Recipe (Serves 4, Preparation Time: 6 minutes)

Ingredients:

- 4 salmon fillets
    - 1 tablespoon olive oil
    - 1/3 cup brown sugar
    - 3 tablespoons Asian fish sauce
    - 2 tablespoons lime juice
    - 1 1/2 tablespoons low-sodium soy sauce
    - 1 teaspoon grated ginger

- 1 teaspoon lime zest
- 1/2 teaspoon ground black pepper
- Fresh cilantro and green onions for garnish

Instructions:

1. In sauté mode, combine brown sugar, olive oil, fish sauce, soy sauce, lime juice, black pepper, lime zest, and grated ginger. Let the mixture simmer.
2. Place the salmon fillets in the Instant Pot with the skin side up. Pour the sauce over the salmon using a spoon.
3. Cook under low pressure for 1 minute.
4. Carefully transfer the salmon to a serving dish, ensuring the caramelized side is facing up.
5. Continue sautéing the remaining sauce in the pot until it thickens into a syrup.
6. Pour the thickened sauce over the salmon and garnish with fresh cilantro and green onions.

—-

4.5 Mung Bean Pudding Recipe (Serves 6, Preparation Time: 20 minutes)

Ingredients:

- 2/3 cup split mung beans
    - 1/4 cup sticky rice
    - 4 1/2 cups water
    - A pinch of salt

- 1/4 cup sugar
- Coconut milk for serving

Instructions:

1. Wash and drain the mung beans and sticky rice.
2. Add them to the Instant Pot with water and a pinch of salt.
3. Cook under high pressure for 2 minutes.
4. Switch the pot to sauté mode.
5. Prepare a starch slurry by mixing starch and water. Gradually add it to the mung bean mixture, stirring continuously until the desired thickness is achieved.
6. The pudding will thicken as it cools down.
7. Mix in sugar to taste.
8. Serve the pudding topped with coconut milk.

6

Chapter 5: Korean Instant Pot Recipes

5.1 Instant Pot Soup Recipes (2 Recipes)

We are now delving into a cuisine that might intrigue you the most when it comes to experimenting with your Instant Pot. Rest assured, the simplicity of creating these dishes will surprise you.

Galbitang Soup

Ingredients:

- 1.5 pounds beef short ribs
    - 8 cups water
    - 1 yellow onion (with skin on)
    - 2 green onions (2 for broth, 2 for garnish)
    - 2 slices of ginger
    - 1/2 Korean radish (cut into big chunks)
    - 2 tablespoons chopped garlic

- 2 teaspoons Guk ganjang
- 1 teaspoon Korean Cheonilyeom Salt

Instructions:

1. Trim excess fat from ribs and rinse with cold water.
2. Clean and chop green onions and Korean radish.
3. In the pot, add whole yellow onion, ribs, green onions, ginger, and radish. Add plenty of water.
4. Set the pot to soup function and pressure cook for 30 minutes.
5. Release pot pressure, remove excess fat from the soup.
6. Season with Guk ganjang, garlic, and salt.

Kimchi Jjigae

Ingredients:

- 2 cups kimchi
    - 1 pound beef cubes (cut into 2-inch cubes)
    - 1 cup diced onion
    - 1 cup dried shiitake mushrooms
    - 1 tablespoon minced garlic
    - 1 tablespoon minced ginger
    - 1 tablespoon sesame oil
    - 1 tablespoon dark soy sauce
    - 1 tablespoon Gochugaru
    - 1 tablespoon Gochujang
    - 1/4 teaspoon Splenda
    - 2 cups water

- Kosher salt

Instructions:

1. Combine all ingredients in the pot.
2. Pressure cook on high for 15 minutes.
3. Add diced tofu and green onions if desired.
4. Kimchi Jjigae is ready to serve.

Korean Pulled Pork

Ingredients:

- 4 pieces boneless pork shoulder
    - 4 cloves minced garlic
    - 1/2 cup soy sauce
    - 1/2 cup Gochujang sauce
    - 1/2 cup brown sugar
    - 2 tablespoons rice vinegar
    - 2 tablespoons sesame oil
    - 1 tablespoon lime zest
    - 1 tablespoon lime juice
    - 2 teaspoons grated ginger
    - 1 tablespoon cornstarch
    - 2 tablespoons cornstarch (for sauce thickening)
    - Rice for serving
    - Garnishes: lime zest, green onions, peanuts

Instructions:

1. Mix soy sauce, brown sugar, sesame oil, lime zest, ground ginger, lime juice, garlic, Gochujang sauce, and rice vinegar to prepare a sauce.
2. Sear pork in sauté mode, turning every few minutes.
3. Pour sauce over pork.
4. Pressure cook for 45 minutes.
5. Remove pork and pull with two forks.
6. In sauté mode, reduce sauce to desired consistency.
7. Serve pulled pork topped with the sauce, with a side of rice.

Dae Ji Bulgogi

Ingredients:

- 1 pound boneless pork shoulder
    - 1 sliced onion
    - 1 tablespoon minced ginger
    - 1 tablespoon minced garlic
    - 1 tablespoon soy sauce
    - 1 tablespoon rice wine
    - 1 tablespoon sesame oil
    - 2 packets Splenda
    - 2 tablespoons Gochujang
    - 1/4-1 teaspoon Gochugaru
    - 1/4 cup water

Instructions:

1. In the Instant Pot, combine all cooking and marinating ingredients. Let it marinate for 24 hours.
2. Pressure cook for 20 minutes.
3. In a wide iron pan, sauté onion slices and pork cubes.
4. Add 1/2 or 1/4 cup of sauce. Caramelize sauce on high heat until it coats the meat.
5. Top with green onions, sesame seeds, and serve.
6. Serve leftover sauce as a side.

Korean Chicken

Ingredients:

- 1 pound boneless chicken thighs (bite-size pieces)
    - 1 diced onion
    - 1/2 cup soy sauce
    - 1/2 cup chicken broth
    - 1 tablespoon garlic
    - 4 tablespoons brown sugar
    - 1-3 teaspoons Sriracha
    - 1/4 teaspoon Hoisin sauce
    - 1 teaspoon minced ginger
    - 1 tablespoon cornstarch (plus 2 tablespoons for thickening)

Instructions:

1. Put chicken and onion in Instant Pot.
2. Mix all ingredients except 1 tablespoon of cornstarch and add to Instant Pot.
3. Pressure cook for 5 minutes.
4. If thicker sauce is desired, mix some warm liquid from the pot with 2 tablespoons cornstarch until smooth. Add to boiling pot contents.
5. Cook for 1 minute, let rest for 5 minutes.
6. Garnish with sesame seeds. Serve with rice.

Anchovy Stock

Ingredients:

- 1 ounce dried anchovies
  - 4 cups cold tap water
  - 3 small pieces of Kombu (kelp)

Instructions:

1. Place a pound of anchovies and 4 cups of water into the Instant Pot.
2. Seal the lid and pressure cook the mixture for at least 5 minutes.
3. Strain the steaming fish sauce into a separate container.
4. Add Kombu to the sauce.
5. Let it cool and store it in the refrigerator.
6. Remove the Kombu after 12 hours.

Jjamppong

Ingredients:

- 8 ounces Korean noodles
    - 2 tablespoons cooking oil
    - 3 cloves minced garlic
    - 1/2 small onion
    - 8 ounces medium-sized shrimp
    - 12 ounces Manila clams
    - 4 ounces squid
    - 4 ounces bay scallops
    - 4 tablespoons Gochujang
    - 1 tablespoon Gochugaru (powdered chili)
    - 4 cups chicken broth
    - 4 ounces Napa cabbage
    - 4 ounces Bok Choy
    - 1-2 tablespoons soy sauce
    - Salt to taste
    - 2 stalks scallions

Instructions:

1. Heat the Instant Pot in sauté mode and add oil.
2. Once hot, add onion and garlic, sauté until fragrant.
3. Add clams, shrimp, scallops, squid, Gochujang, and powdered chili. Mix well.
4. Pour in the chicken stock, then add Bok Choy and Napa cabbage. Let the soup boil, then add salt, soy sauce, and noodles.
5. Cook for 30 seconds.
6. Garnish with scallions and serve hot.

Korean Sticky Rice

Ingredients:

- 2 cups sweet rice
    - 1 cup water
    - 1/2 cup brown sugar
    - 2 tablespoons soy sauce
    - 2 tablespoons sesame oil
    - 1/2 cup dried jujube dates
    - 1 tablespoon pine nuts
    - 13 ounces chestnuts

Instructions:

1. Soak the rice in water for 6 hours, then rinse and drain.
2. Separate the flesh from the jujube dates and cut it into small pieces.
3. Add sesame oil to the Instant Pot to coat its base.
4. Add the drained rice, sugar, water, and soy sauce. Mix well.
5. Add jujube dates, chestnuts, and pine nuts.
6. Close the lid and pressure cook on low for 8 minutes.
7. Stir the sticky rice with a wooden spoon until the mixture is uniform.
8. Serve the sticky rice as it is or shape it using a cupcake mold.

7

In summary:

Considering the diverse culinary traditions discussed earlier, we can now categorize them collectively as Asian cuisine. Asian food varies significantly across different regions – North, Central, East, and West Asian cuisines each possess distinct characteristics. While rice serves as a universal ingredient, its type also differs across Asian regions. For example, Basmati rice is common in India, whereas Jasmine Rice is prevalent in Southeast Asia. One remarkable feature of Asian cuisine is its ability to balance salt and sugar in savory dishes. The recipes mentioned encompass culinary delights from diverse Asian cultures like India, Korea, Vietnam, China, and Thailand. Despite their differences, what unites these recipes is the ease with which they can be prepared using the Instant Pot. As discussed earlier in this book, the Instant Pot proves indispensable for both beginners and experienced cooks seeking an authentic Asian culinary experience. Therefore, it stands as a essential kitchen tool for anyone wanting to enjoy the rich flavors of Asian cuisine.

www.ingramcontent.com/pod-product-compliance
Lightning Source LLC
LaVergne TN
LVHW020422080526
838202LV00055B/5001